GENERAL ELEMENTS OF LIABILITY -

Exam Reference: H418/01 – The Legal System and Criminal Law (Paper 1)
Actus reus is a substantive topic that appears in paper 1 of the OCR Law A-Level allocated to substantive law topics in this paper. You will be required to accurately principles of actus reus in relation to a variety of offences.

Topic Content:
- Actus reus:
- Conduct; acts and omissions and state of affairs
- Voluntariness and involuntariness
- Causation
- Consequences

Topic introduction

The criminal law is a broad and diverse area of law which contains thousands of different criminal offences that vary significantly in terms of seriousness, ranging for murder to minor regulatory offences e.g., speeding.

The criminal law is not consolidated, this means that it is not all contained within one place, rather we get our law of crime from a variety of different sources. The majority of criminal offences are defined in either an Act of Parliament, or, by the common law and thus established in the judgment of a case.

Generally (whilst remembering in law that there are always exceptions), each criminal offence will have a definition of the actions and/or conduct that must be proved in order for the defendant to be guilty, this is known as the **actus reus**. The definition will also usually outline the state of mind that the defendant must have had at the time of carrying out the actus reus in order to be found guilty, this is known as the **mens rea**. Therefore, generally, each crime has two distinguishable parts, the guilty act that must be proved, and the guilty mind that must accompany the guilty act of the defendant, in order for them to be found guilty.

Key Terms:

Actus reus: The guilty act.

Mens rea: The guilty mind.

In order for a defendant to be prosecuted and found guilty of a crime they must have both the actus reus and mens rea.

In simple terms they must have committed the specified criminal act with the requisite criminal mind.

Actus Reus

The two general principles of actus reus:

1. The defendant must commit the actus reus **voluntarily**
2. The defendant must commit the offence via a **positive action**

There are exceptions to both of these principles.

> **Exam Gold** In scenario questions, when applying criminal offences, you do not need to refer to the two general principles of criminal liability every single time, rather, you discuss them when it appears that there is some aspect of these principles in dispute. E.g., you would only discuss the voluntary principle where it appears the defendant did not commit the offence voluntarily. You may do so in conjunction with the defence of automatism.

1 The voluntary principle

In order for actus reus to be proved, it must be proved that the guilty act was a voluntary action of the defendant. If the defendant has not carried out his actions voluntarily, the courts may not find them guilty of committing the offence, as their actus reus was not voluntary. There is a subtle distinction here, but it is important to distinguish the concept of voluntariness from mens rea.

Key Case
Hill v Baxter (1958)

Facts: The defendant drove across a road junction, ignoring an illuminated 'halt' sign and hit another car. The defendant was in a confused condition after the incident and had no recollection of it occurring. There was no medical explanation for this confusion or memory loss.

Outcome: Guilty

Legal principle: Whilst the defendant in this case was found guilty, the judges outlined circumstances where a defendant would be in a state of automatism, not acting voluntarily and therefore not guilty of an offence. These circumstances included, if whilst driving, a defendant suffered a stroke or epileptic fit, if they were hit on the head by a stone or attacked by a swarm of bees.

Example: Ahmed and Amira

Ahmed was playing on a zipwire at his local park with his friends, who were stood close by taking pictures. As Ahmed got to the end of the zipwire the wire snapped and sent him flying towards his friend Amira. Ahmed knocked Amira over and she suffered a sprained wrist. Ahmed would not be guilty of a crime here, his actions were not voluntary, they were caused by the faulty wire, further he had no mens rea in relation to Amira.

The exception: State of affairs offences

Whilst it is a general principle of actus reus that the guilty act must be a voluntary action of the defendant, there is an exception to this rule, it does not conclusively apply to all criminal offences.

There exists a category of offences known as 'state of affairs offences', these include a small range of crimes, whereby a defendant satisfies the actus reus of the crime by being in a certain 'state of affairs', this means being at a particular place at a particular time, even where they were not there voluntarily. Proof of those particular circumstances satisfies the actus reus, irrelevant of whether the defendant demonstrated voluntarily fault getting there. The existence of these offences is justified upon the grounds that, however a defendant got there, such circumstances are so dangerous to others or demonstrate such fault that a criminal prosecution is justified.

Key Case
Winzar v Chief Constable of Kent (1983)

Facts: The police were called to remove an intoxicated defendant from a hospital. The police placed the defendant inside their vehicle outside of the hospital and charged him with being drunk on the highway.

Outcome: Guilty

Legal principle: The elements of this offence required proof that the defendant was drunk on the highway as a question of fact, nothing further.

2 The actus reus must be a positive action

The second general principle of actus reus requires that the actus reus of an offence must be satisfied by an 'act', a positive physical action by the defendant. This means that the defendant must have undertaken an action under in order to satisfy the offence. Actus reus generally cannot be proved via inaction. Therefore generally, an offence cannot be committed by a mere omission (a failure to act).

The criminal law generally prohibits certain acts that if proved amount to criminal offences, usually, the criminal law does not impose obligations to act and then punish for any inaction.

OCR A-LEVEL LAW

CRIMINAL LAW
STUDY BOOK 1

Authors:
Liz Nuttall *and*
Sarah Sharp

tutor2u

Student Name:

ABOUT THIS STUDY BOOK

This tutor2u OCR A-Level Law study book provides a comprehensive set of essential study notes on Criminal Law which is assessed in Paper 1 of the OCR Law A-Level exam series. This study book is part 1 of a 2 book bundle.

We've broken down each section into:
- Specification links; Exam reference and topic content
- Complete, concise notes on each topic including relevant statutes, case law and examples
- Exam gold – advice from experienced examiners about common student misconceptions and what to focus on in your revision
- Theory links – linking substantive topics to overarching legal theory
- Key terms glossaries – consolidating each chapter with a definition of the important topic terminology
- Case summary tables – summarising each chapter with a quick reference review of the key cases with topic links and legal significance of each case

Make this study book your own. Highlight and annotate key points. Add your own comments and examples to make the notes invaluable for your exam revision.

STUDY BOOK 1 CONTENTS

GENERAL ELEMENTS OF LIABILITY - ACTUS REUS	Page 3
GENERAL ELEMENTS OF LIABILITY - MENS REA	Page 20
FATAL OFFENCES AGAINST THE PERSON - MURDER	Page 32
FATAL OFFENCES AGAINST THE PERSON - VOLUNTARY MANSLAUGHTER	Page 38
FATAL OFFENCES AGAINST THE PERSON - INVOLUNTARY MANSLAUGHTER	Page 54
NON-FATAL OFFENCES AGAINST THE PERSON	Page 70

Example: Sandia the Bystander

Sandia was walking around a reservoir, as she every Sunday morning. On this particular morning, Sandia noticed that there was a child struggling to stay afloat in the water. Sandia, who has a fear of water herself, walked on past and the child drowned.

Sandia's actions would not amount to the actus reus of a crime as this is known as a 'pure omission', she did not cause the child to in the river, or have any link to them, so bears no liability as a mere bystander.

The exceptions: Omissions:

Whilst the general principle is that the actus reus of a crime cannot be satisfied by inaction, a failure to act, there are two exceptions to this rule.

In other words, there are two ways that a defendant can commit an offence via omission, two circumstances where the actus reus of an offence can be satisfied by inaction on the part of the defendant, otherwise known as a failure to act.

1. Where Parliament have created an offence which criminalises a specific failure to act e.g., if without reasonable excuse, a defendant fails to co-operate with a preliminary roadside breath test is an offence under **s6(6) Road Traffic Act 1988**.

2. Where the law recognises that the defendant is under a duty to act and they fail to act, this inaction can form the actus reus of a criminal offence, even where there is no reference in the definition of the crime to any 'failure to act'. If there is no duty to act, the inaction cannot constitute the actus reus of a criminal offence.

> **Exam Gold** In a scenario question the law of omissions may feature as a question on its own or as part of an offence, where the defendant has committed the actus reus of the offence via a failure to act, by not acting, not intervening, rather than doing something that constitutes / causes actus reus. Most fatal and non-fatal offences can be committed by omission. The only exceptions to this rule are the offences of assault and unlawful act manslaughter, both require proof of an act and therefore cannot be committed by omission.

The common law recognises six duties to act:

1. A duty specified in a **contract of employment:** a person's contract of employment may specify that particular duties have to be undertaken to a particular standard, which, if the defendant fails to complete may form the actus reus of an offence.

Key Case
R v Adomako (1994)

Facts: The defendant was an anaesthetist employed by a hospital. His contractual role was to safely provide anaesthesia and pain relief to patients during operations. During one operation the defendant failed to notice that a patient's breathing tube had become disconnected, once alerted to an issue he failed to check the tube as a competent anaesthetist would have done and the patient died.

Outcome: Guilty

Legal principle: His failure to adequately perform his duties satisfied the actus reus of gross negligence manslaughter because he was under a contractual duty to act.

2. A duty because of a **relationship**: generally, only a parent – child relationship will suffice. Other relationships do not tend to automatically impose a duty to act from one party to another.

Key Case
R v Gibbins and Proctor (1918)

Facts: Mr Gibbin's wife had left him resulting in him and his daughter, Nelly aged 7, moving in with another woman, Proctor. The family had sufficient funds to support all residing within the house, but Nelly was deliberately starved which caused her death. The defendants then hid the child's body and buried it in a brickyard in order to conceal her death. The two defendants were charged with her murder.

Outcome: Guilty

Legal principle: The defendants were guilty of murder by omission, the father was under a duty to act based upon the familial relationship. Proctor was also acting as a parent as in reality she was undertaking the role of the child's mother.

Example: Cousins

Iris and Anna were cousins who did not speak due to their immediate families not getting on. Iris was walking home from a night out and saw Anna passed in an alleyway, unconscious and vomiting. Anna choked on her own vomit and died as no-one was aware she was there and in distress.

Iris would not be guilty of committing a crime by omission by not helping Anna or alerting the emergency services as she does not have a sufficiently close relationship with Anna for a duty of care to be imposed; she also played no other causative role in Anna being in this dangerous position.

3. A duty which is **assumed through acceptance of care**: where one party assumes care and responsibility for another who is dependent upon them, with voluntarily or due to the circumstances of living, this may lead to the imposition of a duty to act. Where such a duty to act is imposed, any failure to act can amount to the actus reus of a criminal offence.

Key Case
R v Instan (1893)

Facts: The defendant was the niece of the victim (her aunt), who provided the defendant with accommodation and support. The Aunt began to suffer from gangrene and was unable to call for medical help or look after herself. The defendant (niece), the only person with knowledge of this, failed to give her aunt any food or assistance, or alert anyone else to the severe nature of the situation. The Aunt died from the gangrene and the defendant was charged with gross negligence manslaughter.

Outcome: Guilty

Legal principle: The defendant (niece) was under a duty to act as she had assumed responsibility for the aunt by continuing to live in her house and be financially supported by her, she was further the only one aware of the condition of the aunt. The failure to act formed the actus reus of manslaughter. Whilst the gangrene was the cause of the death, the defendants' actions accelerated the time of her death and was thus a contributory factor.

Example: Next Door Neigbours

Tariq, a married man, lived with his wife and son. Next door to Tariq, lived Egbert, an elderly gentleman who had no family to care for him. For over a year Tariq had checked on Egbert every day and brought him groceries and his medicine. Tariq's wife gave birth to his second child and Tariq stopped checking on Egbert. Tariq noticed that he had not seen Egbert for a couple of weeks but did nothing. Egbert was later found dead.

The courts may find Tariq guilty of gross negligence manslaughter on the basis that he owed a duty of care to Egbert because he voluntarily assumed responsibility for him. Thus, the omission to continue to act could form the actus reus of the offence.

4. A duty to act because the defendant has **created a dangerous situation**: this arises where the defendant sets in a motion a dangerous series of events. Where they fail to prevent harm or damage occurring as a result of their actions, this failure to act can form the actus reus of a criminal offence.

Key Case
R v Evans (2009)

Facts: The victim, a heroin addict was given heroin by her sister and mother (the defendants), then self-injected the heroin whilst residing in her mother's house. It became clear that the victim was suffering from an overdose, but the defendants chose not to seek medical assistance for fear of discovery of the drugs and simply put the victim to bed. The two defendants went to sleep in the same room as her. They both awoke the next day to find that the victim had died and were both prosecuted for gross negligence manslaughter.

Outcome: Guilty

Legal principle: The mother was under a duty to act as the victim's parent, however, the sister owed a duty of care to her sister, not due to her family relationship with victim, but rather because she created or contributed to the creation of a dangerous situation which she knew, or ought reasonably to know had become life threatening. The sister was under a duty to take reasonable steps for the safety of the victim once she appreciated that the heroin she procured for her was having a potentially fatal impact on her health.

5. A duty towards the victim due to **public duty from an official position**. Where the defendant holds an official position, such as being a police officer, this can provide a duty to act. In contrast to a mere bystander the officer must act. Failure to do so can become the actus reus of a crime.

Key Case
R v Dytham (1979)

Facts: The defendant (a police officer), witnessed the victim being beaten and kicked to death by a bouncer outside a nightclub. The defendant failed to intervene or request help and left the scene as his shift was due to end. The defendant was charged with misconduct in a public office.

Outcome: Guilty

Legal principle: The defendant was under a public duty to act due to his official position. The court held that a police officer has a duty of care to all of society and must not fail to fulfil this duty by act or omission. The crime of misconduct in a public office can be committed via an omission.

6. A duty can also arise because of a **combination of factors based on public policy:** the law has recognised in some circumstances that a duty to act may arise because of the combined presence of multiple factors including through complicity in a crime:

Key Case
R v Willoughby (2005)

Facts: The defendant was the owner of a disused pub. One evening a fire begun and destroyed the premises and killed the victim. It was alleged that the defendant and victim had started the fire at the premises deliberately, because the defendant was in debt with two mortgages on the property. The defendant, who was found with petrol in his car was prosecuted for gross negligence manslaughter.

Outcome: Guilty

Legal principle: The defendant owed a duty of care to the victim, not just because he was the owner of the premises, but because in addition to this, the venture was for the defendant's financial gain, the victim was enlisted by the defendant, and he was undertaking the dangerous task of pouring the petrol inside. This combination of factors gave rise to a duty to act in the common law.

Causation

When looking at the actus reus of a criminal offence, usually found in either a statute or the common law, it is important to pay close attention to the nature of the offence. The description of the actus reus may either specify a particular type of conduct / behaviour that must be proved, without the causing of any particular consequence. Alternatively, the actus reus may require proof of the causing of a particular result, without specifying exactly what actions have to be proved to have caused that result, rather the causing of the consequence is criminalised.

The distinction between the two types of actus reus in this way is important, because essentially there exist two types of offences according to the nature of the actus reus; result crimes or conduct crimes. This distinction is important because result crimes are subject to a body of principles called causation, whereas conduct crimes are not.

Result crime	The actus reus of a result crime specifies the causing of a particular criminal result as the guilty act. *Examples: murder, involuntary manslaughter, grievous bodily harm / wounding with intent (s18), grievous bodily harm / wounding (s20), assault occasioning actual bodily harm*
Conduct crime	The actus reus of a conduct crime specifies the undertaking of a particular behaviour or action as the guilty act; there is no need to prove that any particular result occurred as a consequence of the conduct, merely that the guilty conduct did itself occur. *Examples: attempts, being drunk on a public highway, dangerous driving, speeding, theft, making off without payment.*

Exam Gold WWhen studying criminal offences, it is important to understand which are result crimes and which are conduct crimes. Result crimes require causation to be satisfied. For conduct crimes the causation principles are not applicable.

For result crimes, in addition to proving that the victim has suffered the particular type of result specified, you have to prove that the defendant caused that result. You establish that the defendant caused the result by proving two types of causation. So, for these offences, not only must the result required for the particular offence be proved, but it must also be proved that the defendant was a cause of that result, in fact and by law. The two types of causation that must be proved are therefore known as **factual** and **legal** causation.

It is often assumed that in order for the defendant to be regarded as the cause of the result that they must be the only or main cause, that is not the case, a defendant will be regarded the cause where both factual and legal causation are proved, irrelevant of the number of other causes or parties that have contributed toward the outcome.

1 Factual causation: the 'but for' test

In order to establish the 'but for' test the courts will ask 'But for the defendant's actions, would the criminal consequence have occurred?'

> ⭐ **Exam Gold** In an application question, when applying factual causation, you should always re-phrase the 'but for' test to reflect the context of the scenario presented, so always cite the question above but state what the defendants' actions were and what the criminal consequence is as relevant to the offence you are discussing. For example, if Adam shot Ben in the head and Ben died, you would ask 'but for Adam shooting Ben in the head would Ben have died?'

Yes: if the criminal consequence (actus reus) would have occurred anyway despite the defendant's actions he is **NOT** regarded as the factual cause, his action or inaction has therefore had no effect on the outcome, that outcome which would have occurred anyway.

No: if the criminal result (actus reus) would not have occurred 'but for' the defendant's actions he **WILL** be regarded as the factual cause, this is because that causing of the actus reus is directly linked to the defendant's actions as it would not have occurred without them.

Key Case
R v White (1910)

Facts: Mrs White (the victim) was found deceased on her sofa in her home. Near the sofa was a glass containing a drink which was later discovered to contain potassium cyanide, a fatal poison where ingested in large doses. The post-mortem examination determined that the death was due to a heart attack, not caused by the potassium cyanide, and that in any case, there was not sufficient cyanide in the drink to cause the death of the victim. The victim's son (the defendant) was proved to have purchased the cyanide and have motive for causing his mother's death and was charged with her murder.

Outcome: Not guilty of murder, guilty of attempted murder

Legal principle: The defendant could not be convicted of the murder of his mother as factually his actions, despite his intent, did not cause her death as but for him poisoning her drink, her death would have occurred anyway, irrelevant of his actions.

2 Legal causation

Once factual causation has been established, legal causation must then be proved. Factual causation establishes as a question of fact that they defendant's actions and the criminal result are linked, but this alone is not sufficient to establish liability.

In order to establish that the defendant is a legal cause of the criminal result it must be proved that the defendants' actions were an operating cause of the outcome. For many years the phrase 'operating and substantial' was cited within this context, however, it has long been established that for legal causation to be proved the defendant's contribution does not need to be proved as substantial.

In the case of **R v Cheshire (1991)** the court held that '… the accused's acts need not be the sole cause or even the main cause of death, it being sufficient that his acts contributed significantly to that result.'

Key Case
R v Kimsey (1996)

Facts: The defendant and victim had been involved in a high-speed car chase which caused the death of the victim. The prosecution and defence had varying accounts about the specific order of events that led to the victim's death. The prosecution alleged that the defendant had overtaken the victim and struck her car, which then caused her to lose control of the car, following which she was struck by another car and killed. The defence case was that the victim had lost control of her car, struck the car of the defendant, and then subsequently was hit by the third-party car and killed. The defendant was convicted of causing death by dangerous driving.

Outcome: Guilty

Legal principle: Whilst juries are often advised that the defendant must be a substantial cause of the result for legal causation to be satisfied, it is not in fact essential to prove that the defendant was the principal, or a substantial, cause of the death, as long as the jury is sure that the defendant's actions were a cause and that there was something more than a slight or a trifling link between the defendant's actions and the criminal consequence.

Novus actus interveniens (new intervening acts)

In addition to require proof that the defendant's actions contributed in more than a slight or trifling way to the result, legal causation also considers the effect of other contributory factors on the defendant's liability. This involves looking at the chain of causation, in other words, the chain of events between the defendants' actions and the criminal result that has occurred. A defendant may not be regarded as the 'operating and substantial' cause of the result because the actions of another or some other factor has intervened between their actions and the prohibited consequence, usually rendering the harm to the victim significantly worse. The courts have developed various legal test to determine whether such intervention will prevent any liability of the defendant for the further harm that is suffered by the victim. Anything that does occur between the actions of the defendant and the final criminal consequence, if proved as breaking the chain are known as a **'novus actus interveniens'**.

Novus actus interveniens *translates as 'new intervening acts', in some circumstances intervening acts may break the chain of causation meaning that the defendant is no longer regarded as the legal cause of the result and therefore no longer guilty of the offence.*

For example, in a murder case, it may be the case that where, even though the first defendant has started a chain of events which has led to the victim's death, if other more serious contributory factors occurred after that of the first defendant, this may mean that the first defendant should no longer be held liable for the final outcome. Alternatively, the courts may use legal causation to establish that even though something has occurred between the actions of the defendant and the victim's death, that the further action was minor and thus the chain of causation is unbroken, the chain of fault and liability is evidenced and not disturbed. Where proved, the defendant is regarded as an operating cause of the result, established via an unbroken chain of causation, and thus has caused the actus reus of the offence.

It is important to note that where there is a first defendant who has some casual role in causing a criminal consequence, along with a second defendant who plays a causal role, sometimes the courts may find them both liable, it is not the case that in result crimes only one defendant may be prosecuted.

> **Exam Gold** In an application question, the amount of time that you dedicate the topic of causation will depend upon if the scenario presents any causation issues. Where causation is clearly easily satisfied, you should aim to cover it in only a few sentences. An examiner will not give credit for covering the topic in-depth where there is little included in the scenario for discussion.

> **Example: Doctors New Interveening Act**
> Yasmin punched Kesha causing Kesha to suffer a severe headache. Kesha chose to attend her nearest A&E department. The doctor ordered a CT scan, but then failed to review it properly because the doctor was under the influence of illegal drugs whilst working. This resulted in a severe bleed on the brain being missed. Shortly after, Kesha died. The courts may determine that Yasmin is not responsible for the murder / manslaughter of Kesha, as the chain has been broken by the incompetence and negligence of the doctor (who may be separately prosecuted for gross negligence manslaughter). In these circumstances Yasmin would likely still be prosecuted for a non-fatal offence against Kesha in regard to the initial injury she caused her.

Over time the law has recognised different categories of novus actus interveniens and developed different tests to determine when actions within each of the categories will or will not break the causal chain.

1 Third party intervention

In some circumstances a third party, a second party and possibly additional defendant, may contribute toward the final injury suffered by the defendant between the defendant's actions and the final outcome.

Where another party appears to contribute to the overall result there are three possible conclusions the court may come to, the court may hold the actions of the third party have had no effect on the chain of causation and the original defendant is the only cause of the final injury. The court may find that the actions of the third party totally overwhelm the actions of the defendant rendering the defendant no longer liable. Alternatively, the courts may hold that both parties have contributed toward the final outcome, and both may be found liable of the criminal offence.

The test: the actions of a third party will only break the chain of causation where they were sufficiently independent of and unforeseeable in relation the actions of the first defendant.

Example: Third Parties

Defendant attacks the victim with a baseball bat rendering them unconscious with severe injuries.

An accomplice of the defendant kicks the victim multiple times in the head whilst he lays defenceless on the floor, causing further injury.

The victim is found dead later that evening.

In these circumstances the courts would consider the cause of death in line with the post-mortem and the other evidence of the level of injuries. If the victim died from multiple injuries, it is likely that both parties would be found to be causes of the victim's death, particularly as they were accomplices.

Key Case
R v Pagett (1983)

Facts: The defendant, aged 31, had left his wife and formed a relationship with a 16-year-old girl, Gail Kinchen (the victim.) She became pregnant with his child and when six months pregnant left the defendant due to a number of domestic upsets and returned to her family home. The defendant took the victim hostage and drove her to his flat followed by the police. Following a long negotiation between the defendant and police, the defendant opened the flat door with the victim in front of him, using her as a shield, in a dimly light hallway he shot at the police officers who returned fire, the victim was killed, and the defendant merely harmed. The defendant was prosecuted for the manslaughter of the victim, upon the basis that his actions in shooting at the police and using her a shield were a cause of her death, irrelevant of the fact that it was the police who fired the shots that actually killed her.

Outcome: Guilty

Legal principle: It has long been accepted in law that the mere presence of an intervening act of another person is not enough to break the chain of causation, but that act must be free, deliberate, informed and so independent of the act of the accused that it should be regarded in law as the cause of the victim's death, to the exclusion of the act of the accused. Here the Police officers' actions were performing their lawful duty in relation to the criminal actions of the defendant and thus were not free or independent.

Exam Gold In a scenario question you may have two defendants who have both caused a particular result, for example, two defendants who have contributed toward the death of the victim. The question may ask you to determine any liability of one or both of the defendants. Where this occurs, you will have to consider the effect of each defendant on the chain of causation for the other defendant. Drawing out the events in a brief timeline on the exam paper can often help you to visualise and understand the order of the events.

2 Poor medical treatment

Many criminal cases occur where a defendant injures a victim and as a direct consequence of that injury, they require medical treatment. This quite common occurrence becomes problematic where exceptionally, the medical treatment delivered by professionals fails to adequately treat the patient and in fact causes them to suffer from further harm. The complex question in this case is who should bare liability? The original defendant for starting this chain of events which caused treatment to be necessary? Or the medical practitioner who has failed to fully their own duty properly?

There have been many cases upon circumstances like these, not only in the context of criminal causation but also within the body of law that is medical negligence. Within the context of legal causation, the law has been reluctant to develop a specific test to apply to all cases, possibly to reflect the complex nature of such cases but also to protect medical professionals from bearing the weight of injury preventing criminals at fault from being liable.

Whilst there exists no definitive test, the long chronology of cases demonstrates that treatment provided that is simply bad, or poor is not sufficient enough to break the chain of causation.

The test: negligent medical treatment will only break the chain of causation where it is so overwhelmingly bad that it renders the defendant's original actions so insignificant that it has clearly become the cause of the final injury.

Example: Poor medical treatment

| The defendant stabs the victim in the arm which only causes a superficial, non-life threatening, injury. | The victim attends hospital to have the wound seen to. The nurse checks the victim's medical records and misreads the warning not to administer penicillin. The nurse gives penicillin through an IV whilst the victim is resting and leaves him alone where he suffers a severe allergic reaction and dies. | The nurse returns to find that the victim has suffered a severe seizure and died. |

In these circumstances the courts would consider the cause of death in line with the post-mortem, providing that it is confirmed that the initial wound was only minor, and the death was caused by the seizure in relation to the allergy. The poor medical treatment is likely to break the chain of causation due to extreme nature of the reaction.

Key Case
R v Smith (1959)

Facts: A fight developed in soldier's barracks, the defendant stabbed the victim, who later died. After the incident a colleague carried the victim from the barracks to the medical station and the victim was dropped three times on the way. The medical staff did not correctly assess the severity of the victim's injuries, they were unaware of the stab wound on his back and he died one hour after attending the medical station. The defendant contended that he was not the cause of death as the treatment the victim received was 'thoroughly bad', his estimated chance of recovery if treated correctly was 75%.

Outcome: Guilty

Legal principle: If at the time of death, the original wound is still an operating cause and a substantial cause, then the death was caused by the wound, irrelevant of the fact that some other cause of death is also present. Only, if the second cause is so overwhelming as to make the original wound merely part of the history can it be said that the wound has not caused the death.

Key Case
R v Cheshire (1991)

Facts: Late at night the defendant and victim became involved in a heated argument in a fish and chip shop. The defendant, armed with a shotgun, shot the victim twice. The injuries suffered were severe and after extensive surgery the victim remained in intensive care on a ventilator, this was later replaced with a tracheotomy tube. The victim began to improve but continued to complain of breathing difficulties which were attributed to anxiety. The victim died of complications associated with the tracheotomy tube. By this time the wounds from the gunshots were no longer life-threatening. The victim would likely not have died if the tube complications had been properly assessed. The defendant was charged with murder.

Outcome: Guilty

Legal principle: Even in cases where negligent medical treatment appears to be the immediate cause of the victim's death, this should not prevent the original defendant still being regarded as a cause of death unless the 'negligent treatment was so independent of his acts, and in itself so potent in causing death, that they regard the contribution made by his acts as insignificant'.

> **Exam Gold** In a scenario question it is important to only discuss poor medical treatment where the scenario clearly references medical treatment involving a mistake, misdiagnosis or bad treatment worsening the condition. Many students mistakenly discuss poor medical treatment as soon as there is reference to medical staff, an ambulance or a hospital. Poor medical treatment should only be discussed where there is reference to treatment lower than the expected standard that appears to have contributed to the extent of the injuries suffered by a victim.

In some cases, defendants have sought to establish that even competent medical treatment breaks the chain of causation where it directly precedes the death of the victim.

Key Case
R v Malcherek & Steel (1981)

Facts: This case concerned two appeals on similar facts. Both defendants had been convicted of murder following the carrying out of attacks on their victims who were later found upon medical diagnosis to be brain-dead, the decision was therefore made by medical staff to discontinue life support treatment via the switching off of life support machines. In both trials the issue of causation was not left to the jury to determine. Both appeals contended that the judge should have left the issue of causation to the jury, to determine if the actions of the doctors in turning off the life support machines were in fact the cause of death.

Outcome: Guilty.

Legal principle: The defendant's continued to be the operating cause of death, the withdrawal of life-sustaining treatment does not break the chain of causation between the initial injury and the death.

> **Exam Gold** If you are required to consider causation more than once within a 20-mark scenario question, for example if you have more than one defendant or crime, explain all aspects fully the first time you are applying the principles. The next time you are dealing with causation, you do not need to repeat all the principles again, simply reapply the relevant principles. You will not get double credit for re-explaining the same principles twice and this can waste time in the exam.

3 Actions of the victim

In some cases, after the defendant commits their unlawful acts, the victim may then act in response to those of the defendant and cause their ultimate harm or worsen the extent of the injuries. In these circumstances the defendant may seek to argue that they were therefore not the cause of the injuries the victim has suffered.

The test: the courts will consider within the victim's actions were **reasonably (objectively) foreseeable** within the context of the defendant's actions.

If the victim acts in a foreseeable way in response to the defendant's actions and suffers harm / further harm as a result, this **will not** break the chain of causation.

If the victim acts in an unforeseeable way in response to the defendant's actions and suffers harm / further harm as a result, this **will** break the chain of causation, as the actions cannot be regarded as the fault of the defendant.

Key Case
R v Roberts (1971)

Facts: The defendant offered the victim a lift after a party. The defendant and victim did not know each other. During the car journey the defendant made sexual advances towards the victim and tried removing her coat. This combined with an earlier conversation of concern to the victim, led her to jump out of the moving vehicle whereby she suffered injury. The defendant was consequently convicted of assault occasioning actual bodily harm.

Outcome: Guilty

Legal principle: If a victim does something so daft or unexpected in reaction to the act of a defendant, that defendant cannot be said to have caused it in law, it could not be foreseen by the reasonable man. Here the victim's actions were a reasonably foreseeable consequence of what the defendant was doing, therefore he caused her actions, and the chain of causation was not broken.

This area of law presents an interesting dilemma where the victim actually causes further injury to themselves following the attack of the victim. The courts have to determine if here the victims' actions, which may be argued as unexpected, break the chain of causation.

Key Case
R v Dear (1996)

Facts: The defendant attacked the victim with a knife causing multiple wounds, following an accusation against the victim from his daughter. Two days after the attack, the victim re-opened the wounds and as a consequence died of blood loss. The defendant was prosecuted for murder following his death but argued that his actions amounted to a novus actus interveniens.

Outcome: Guilty

Legal principle: The defendant was still the operating and substantial cause of death as his actions were the only ones that caused the victim to re-open his wounds. The death was caused by the facial injuries originally inflicted by the victim, and thus the attack was still an operating cause of the death. The victim's actions may also be a cause of death, but that does not prevent the defendant's actions still being an operating cause of death.

If, however the victim's action following that of the defendant is neglect, the courts have consistently decided the chain of causation is not broken. This means that where attack by the defendant requires the victim to seek medical assistance, but the victim does not do so; even if the circumstances are such that any reasonable person would have sought medical treatment, this will generally not break the chain of causation.

This is the case even where it may be proved that medical treatment could have prevented the extent of the injury worsening, or even death. The chain remains unbroken, this reflects the fact that the victim retains choice and autonomy over their own body and decision-making. Further, the fault of the injury is caused by the defendant, not the victim. If the courts said that neglect of the victim broke the causal chain, it would place fault upon the decision of the victim when they have been forced to make that decision through the criminal actions of the defendant.

Key Case
R v Holland (1841)

Facts: The defendant attacked the victim causing various injuries, one of particularly severity was a deep cut to the victim's finger. The victim refused amputation of the finger, going against medical advice and later begun to suffer from complications as a direct result of the injury. The victim then agreed to the amputation, but this was too late, and he died as a result of the complications. The defendant sought to argue that the initial refusal of the recommended treatment broke the chain of causation.

Outcome: Guilty

Legal principle: where an initial injury caused by a defendant causes the death of the victim, it is an operating cause of death, it is irrelevant that the death could have been avoided by timely medical treatment.

Exam Gold When applying the principles of legal causation in an exam, you should always begin by explaining what must be proved e.g., the D must be an operating cause of the death and the chain of causation must remain unbroken. If there is a possible novus actus interveniens, reference it from the scenario, identify the category and outline the test and discuss how the facts of the scenario apply to the test, including what the outcome may be. If you are unsure you can speculate, you do not always have to come to a definitive answer. Reasoned conclusions are creditable.

Example: Victims own actions

| The defendant drugs the victim and locks the victim in a room in their flat. | The victim awakes with no recollection of how they came to be in the locked room and can only remember meeting the defendant on a night out and having a drink. The victim realises they are in grave danger and manages to break open a window in the room they are locked in. They jump out of the window which is three floors up. | The victim suffers two broken legs as a result of the jump. |

In these circumstances the courts would consider whether the actions of the victim are reasonably foreseeable. Given the extreme nature of the circumstances that the victim found themselves in, taking extreme measures to escape may be regarded as reasonably foreseeable.

4 Conditions of the victim

In some cases, the extent of the harm suffered by the victim may be much more severe due to a pre-existing condition or circumstances of the victim. In these circumstances, the '**thin skull rule**' *(also referred to as 'eggshell conditions')* applies. According to this rule a defendant '**must take his victim as he finds them**', this means that, if the victim has a particular condition which means that the harm they suffer is worse than the harm a person without that condition would suffer, the defendant is still liable for the full extent of the injuries. The chain of causation is not broken by the condition of the victim.

The thin skull rule applies not only to medical conditions, but also beliefs of the victim. If a victim refuses medical treatment because for example, they believe in alternative holistic treatments over clinical medical treatment, and this results in their death, which could have been avoidable, the chain of causation is not broken.

There are clear policy reasons behind this decision, if the courts said medical conditions broke the chain of causation, then fault is being placed upon the victim for a condition they may have little control over. When a defendant chooses to attack a victim, they should carry the burden of risking them suffering further harm because of their individual conditions, circumstances or beliefs.

Key Case
R v Hayward (1908)

Facts: The defendant husband chased his wife (the victim) down the street whilst continuing to make threats after an argument. The victim fell and was kicked by the defendant and found to be dead. The post-mortem discovered that the victim was suffering from a previously undiagnosed pre-existing gland condition which had caused her death following the physical exertion of running from the defendant. The defendant sought to argue that this broke the chain of causation whereupon he was prosecuted for her manslaughter.

Outcome: Guilty

Legal principle: The defendant's actions remain the operating cause of death even where death is only likely or accelerated due to a pre-existing condition of the victim, whether that condition be known or unknown.

Example: 'Thin skull' conditions

The defendant poisons the victim causing them to suffer severe internal injuries.	Upon admission to hospital the doctors recommend to the victim a course of intrusive medical treatment, without which the poisoning may prove fatal. The victim refuses the medical treatment as they are a strict Christian Scientist who believes in reliance upon God for their healing as opposed to medicine.	The victim dies. It is most likely that they would have survived if they had medical treatment.

In these circumstances although the death of the victim may have been avoidable with medical treatment, this does not break the chain of causation. The right of the victim to refuse treatment is covered within the scope of the thin skull rule. The defendant remains the operating cause of death.

5 A natural event or disaster

Sometimes it will not be the actions of a third person that intervene but what is often described as an 'act of god', a natural event or disaster, which contributes to or causes further harm to the victim.

The test: in these circumstances the courts will consider whether what has occurred is so significant and unforeseeable that it has become the operating cause of criminal consequence, excluding the liability of the defendant. In other words, is the harm now suffered by the victim so significantly different and unforeseeable in relation to the harm caused by the first defendant that it has clearly overwhelmed their actions and become the cause of the result.

Example: Natural event

The defendant and victim, both heavily intoxicated became involved in a fight in a night-club on New Year's Eve. The defendant smashes a glass into the victim's face and neck causing multiple injuries.	An ambulance is called to the scene by security staff who administer first aid to the victim. The ambulance is delayed because there is severe snow causing low visibility.	The ambulance attends the scene and the paramedics recognise that the victim is losing a significant amount of blood. They drive slowly in order to return to hospital but the ambulance skids on ice and crashes, when the paramedics regain consciousness, they find the victim has died from blood loss.

In these circumstances the courts would likely conclude that there is no break in the chain of causation and that the original defendant was the cause of death. The blood loss was caused by the original injuries the victim suffered, and further the weather conditions are a foreseeable occurrence, and ambulance crew demonstrated no fault in driving carefully back to the hospital, the original defendant clearly remains an operating cause of death.

Key Terms – General Elements of Liability: Actus Reus

Actus reus	The physical element of a crime, the conduct, action or consequence that is identified within the definition of a crime.
The voluntary principle	In order for the actus reus of a criminal offence to be proved, it must be established that the actions of the defendant were voluntary.
State of affairs offences	These are offences that criminalises a defendant being found in a particular circumstance at a particular time, irrelevant of how they got there, thus they are an exception to the voluntary principle of actus reus. For example, being drunk on a public highway.
The positive action principle	Generally, in order for the actus reus of an offence to be proved it must be satisfied by a positive action of the defendant, generally an offence cannot be committed by omission. There are exceptions to the principle.
An omission	A failure to act, this will only form the actus reus of a criminal offence where the defendant is under a duty to act.
Conduct crime	A criminal offence where the actus reus requires proof of a particular behaviour or conduct, no outcome to that behaviour needs to be proven in order to satisfy the actus reus. For example, driving without a licence.
Result crime	A criminal offence where the actus reus requires proof of a particular outcome being caused. For these offences both factual and legal causation must be proved in order to find a defendant liable.
Factual causation	Proving causation in fact is established via the 'but for' test, it must be proved that but for the defendant's actions the criminal result would not have occurred.
Legal causation	It must be established that the defendant was an operating cause of the defendant's death, by proving more than a slight or trifling link between their actions and the criminal result, establishing an unbroken chain of causation that is not disrupted by a novus actus interveniens.
Novus actus interveniens	A new intervening act which may break the chain of causation. Generally these acts will only break the chain of causation where they are unforeseeable and significantly independent of the acts of the defendant.

One Sentence Case Summary – General Elements of Liability: Actus Reus		
Name	**Topic Link**	**Legal significance**
Hill v Baxter (1958)	Actus reus – voluntary principle	If a defendant carries out the actus reus of a crime involuntarily, they will not be guilty of the offence, for example, if whilst driving a driver crashed because they suffered a stroke or epileptic fit, or if they were hit on the head by a stone of attacked by a swarm of bees, they would not be guilty of a criminal offence.
Winzar v Chief Constable of Kent (1983)	Actus reus – State of affairs offences	If a defendant is prosecuted for a state of affairs offence, nothing further is required than proof that as a question of fact the state of affairs required by the offence was proved.
R v Adomako (1994)	Actus reus – contractual duty to act	If a contract specifies a particular duty to act and the defendant fails to fulfil that duty, they may commit the actus reus of a criminal offence by omission.
R v Gibbins and Proctor (1918)	Actus reus – duty to act via relationship	If a parent, or stepparent acting as 'loco parentis' fails to adequately care and provide for a child this may form the actus reus of a criminal offence where the child comes to harm, as they owe the child a duty of care.
R v Instan (1893)	Actus reus – duty to act due to assumed responsibility	Where one person assumes or retains responsibility for another a duty to act may be imposed meaning that if that other comes to harm due to the inaction of the defendant, this failure to act may form the actus reus of a criminal offence.
R v Evans (2009)	Actus reus – duty to act due to contribution or creation of a dangerous situation	Where a defendant created or contributed to the creation of a state of affairs which they knew, or ought reasonably to know had become life threatening, any consequential failure to act which results in harm to the victim may form the actus reus of a criminal offence.
R v Dytham (1979)	Actus reus – duty to act due to public duty from an official position	A policer officer has a public duty to act due to his official position. Police officers have a duty of care to all of society and must not fail to fulfil this duty by act or omission.
R v Willoughby (2005)	Actus reus – duty to act due to a combination of factors	In some circumstances a defendant may be under a duty to act due to the combined presence of a number of factors, where proved any following failure to act may form the actus reus of a criminal offence.
R v White (1910)	Actus reus – factual causation	The defendant was not guilty of the murder of his mother by the poisoning of her drink as she did not ingest the poison, but for his actions she would have died, thus factual causation was not satisfied.
R v Kimsey (1996)	Actus reus – legal causation	For legal causation to be satisfied it does not need to be proved that the defendant was the principal, or a substantial, cause of the death, it is enough to prove that there was something more than a slight or a trifling link between the defendant's actions and the criminal consequence.

One Sentence Case Summary – General Elements of Liability: Actus Reus

Name	Topic Link	Legal significance
R v Pagett (1983)	Actus reus – legal causation – third party intervention	Where a third party intervenes in the causal chain between the actions of the first defendant and ultimate outcome, they will only break the causal chain where it is proved they are free, deliberate, informed and so independent of the act of the accused that it should be regarded in law as the cause of the victim's death, to the exclusion of the act of the accused.
R v Smith (1959)	Actus reus – legal causation – poor medical treatment	Poor medical treatment will not break the causal chain where the original injury is still operating at the point of death, only, if the second cause is so overwhelming as to make the original wound merely part of the history can it be said that the initial wound has not caused the death.
R v Cheshire (1991)	Actus reus – legal causation – poor medical treatment	Even in cases where negligent medical treatment appears to be the immediate cause of the victim's death, this should not prevent the original defendant liable unless the 'negligent treatment was so independent of his acts, and in itself so potent in causing death, that they regard the contribution made by his acts as insignificant'.
R v Malcherek & Steel (1981)	Actus reus – legal causation – withdrawal of life-sustaining treatment	Where a defendant injures a victim that requires them to be placed on life support, the defendant will continue to be the operating cause of death, the withdrawal of life-sustaining treatment does not break the chain of causation between the initial injury and the death.
R v Roberts (1991)	Actus reus – legal causation – actions of the victim	If a victim does something so daft or unexpected in reaction to the act of a defendant, the chain of causation will be broken by the victim's acts as they are not objectively foreseeable.
R v Dear (1991)	Actus reus – legal causation – actions of the victim	Where a victim exacerbates injuries caused to themselves by the defendant, this will not break the causal chain where the victim ultimately dies from the injuries that were originally inflicted by the victim, even where worsened by the victim. There are effectively two causes of death.
R v Holland (1841)	Actus reus – legal causation – neglect of the victim	A defendant is not discounted as an operating cause simply because a victim refuses recommend medical treatment, even if this could have avoided the ultimate harm that is caused to the victim. Refusal of medical treatment is not a novus actus interveniens.
R v Hayward (1908)	Actus reus – legal causation – the thin skull rule	The defendant's actions remain the operating cause of death even where death is only likely or accelerated due to a pre-existing condition of the victim, whether that condition be known or unknown.

GENERAL ELEMENTS OF LIABILITY - MENS REA

Exam Reference:	H418/01 – The Legal System and Criminal Law (Paper 1)
	Mens rea is a substantive topic that appears in paper 1 of the OCR Law A-Level exam series. 60 marks out of 80 are allocated to substantive law topics in this paper. You will be required to accurately explain (AO1) and apply (AO2) the different types of mens rea in relation to a variety of offences.
Topic Content:	• Mens rea; intention and subjective recklessness
	• Negligence
	• Transferred malice.
	• No fault: strict liability.
	• Coincidence of actus reus and mens rea

Mens rea

Proving that a defendant is liable for an offence requires proof that not only have they committed the actus reus (the 'guilty act'), but that they also have the relevant mens rea (the 'guilty mind'.) Mens rea requires not that simply at the time of carrying out the actus reus they knew they were committing a criminal offence, in fact knowledge of criminality is not an aspect of mens rea, rather mens rea requires proof of a specific state of mind that the defendant must have had at the time of committing the actus reus.

The particular state of mind, mens rea, that the defendant must have in order to be found guilty of an offence will be specified within the definition of that particular offence. The definitions of criminal offences will either be found in statutes or the common law. The mens rea will usually relate to the extent that the defendant wanted to or realised the risk of the actus reus occurring.

> **Example: Battery**
> The actus reus of battery is the 'application of unlawful force onto the victim', the mens rea is 'intention or recklessness as to the application of unlawful force'. As you can see, the mens rea directly relates to the actus reus. If for example a defendant grabbed the victim from behind, because they genuinely, but mistakenly believed the victim to be someone they knew and looked like, this would unlikely satisfy the mens rea of battery, as there is no intention or recklessness as to unlawful force here.

There are two types of mens rea, namely, intention and recklessness. The definitions of both types of mens rea have been developed by the courts. So, whilst general definitions of these types of mens rea can be applied, what the defendant must have been intending or been reckless in relation to, will be specified within the definition of the criminal offence.

A third area that is considered within the types of mens rea is negligence, negligence is not a type of mens rea per se, but rather an alternative level of fault that can sometimes be required instead of mens rea. The only offence that this relates to in the OCR Criminal Law syllabus is the offence of gross negligence manslaughter, where the offence does not require proof of intention or recklessness in terms of fault, but rather a breach of duty that amounts to gross negligence.

> **Exam Gold** In the exam, mens rea can be featured as a scenario question on its own (as seen in the 2022 exam series) or mens rea may form part of the question. It is typical to consider mens rea after actus reus. As a generic structure for offences, you should generally, identify the offence (always reference where it is contained), then explain and apply the elements of actus reus, explain and apply the mens rea, then, conclude liability, reflecting upon whether all elements of the offences are present to determine whether you have proved in your answer, the likely outcome for the defendant.

It is important to note that mens rea is not the same as, nor is it concerned with motive. A defendant's motive refers to why they wanted to commit the actus reus, their reasons behind the actions. This is different to mens rea which is concerned with whether the defendant wanted to commit the actus reus, not why. A good motive does not automatically mean that a defendant is not guilty of an offence, however, there are some criminal defences which are clearly linked to motive and can render a defendant not guilty if the defence is proved. For example, if a defendant uses force, even lethal force, but is motivated to do so in order to defend themselves or another, this may make the defence of self-defence / defence of another available. Further, the relevance of motive is not totally excluded in the criminal process, it will often be a factor considered when sentencing, depending upon the nature of the motive, becoming either an aggravating or mitigating factor.

Key Case
R v Inglis (2011)

Facts: Following an accident, a young man suffered catastrophic head injuries, his mother attempted to kill her son with a lethal dose of heroin but was unsuccessful. One year later she tried again and this time was successful resulting in the death of her son. She was motivated by a desire to wish to relieve his suffering and prevent a painful death following the withdrawal of life support. She was convicted of both attempted murder and murder.

Outcome: Guilty

Legal principle: The law of murder does not distinguish between defendants who intend to kill out of love or intend to kill out of malice. Whilst motivated by mercy, a mercy killing does not negate the requirements of murder. Motive does not counteract the presence of all elements of the offence.

Exam Gold Whilst mens rea and motive are not the same thing, and a mens rea motivated by factors such as mercy does not prevent mens rea from being present, motive may be evidence of mens rea. For example, if a defendant killed a victim because they had attacked their child, the motive clearly evidences the intention to kill following the attack. So, whilst they are not the same, and motive cannot negate mens rea, motive can be drawn upon as part of your discussion to evidence mens rea.

Types of mens rea

The definitions of criminal offences will clearly specify what state of mind the defendant must have had at the time of carrying out the actus reus in order to be found guilty. Generally, an offence will require either proof of intention or recklessness, so either that the defendant intended to carry out the actus reus, or they were reckless as to whether the actus reus would occur as a consequence of their actions that they intended.

The courts have developed generic definitions of intention and recklessness that can be applied to all criminal offences.

Intention represents a higher level of fault than recklessness. This means that if a defendant has intended the actus reus of an offence to occur they are generally more blameworthy than some-one who has caused the same harm recklessly. This distinction in fault and culpability is often reflected in how offences are categorised, and the sentences attached to them.

Example: Grievous Bodily Harm / Wounding

There are two offences of grievous bodily harm / wounding which have the same actus reus; the defendant has caused either serious harm or a wound to the victim. The first offence is contained within **s20 Offences against the Persons Act 1861** the mens rea for this offence requires proof of intention or recklessness as to some harm, the maximum sentence for which is 5 years imprisonment. **s18** of the same act however, creates a second offence, with the same actus reus, but the mens rea requires proof of intention of serious harm only, the maximum sentence for this offence is life imprisonment. The second offence, despite having the same actus reus as **s20** carries a much harsher sentence to reflect the increased blameworthiness that must be proved for that offence, namely that the defendant acted intentionally, and intended to cause serious harm.

Intention

The common law has recognised two types of intention, namely direct intention and indirect intention. Where a crime requires proof of intention, either of these types of intention will suffice. The common law has further established what must be proved for both types of intent, these definitions can be applied to any offence that references intention within the mens rea.

Direct intention

A defendant directly intends a criminal consequence where they want to carry out the actus reus of a criminal offence, it is what they aim to achieve, their purpose.

Note, whilst 'want' sounds close to our previously discussed concept of 'motive', why the defendant wants to commit the actus reus is irrelevant, direct intention means simply that they wanted to commit it, that it was their aim / desire to commit the actus reus.

R v Mohan (1976) direct intention was defined as the 'decision to bring about the criminal consequence'.

> **Exam Gold** In an exam question whenever you suggest a defendant has a particular type of mens rea (direct intent, indirect intent or recklessness) always begin by defining the type of mens rea with the relevant case, then apply by discussing how the facts appear to demonstrate the defendant made that decision to cause the actus reus, or the extent to which they foresaw it occurring.

Indirect intention

This is also sometimes referred to as 'oblique intention'. The criminal law recognises that sometimes a defendant does not necessarily want an outcome to occur, but the chances of that outcome (the actus reus) occurring are so high, and the defendant realised this and continued with their actions anyway, so that it is only fair to conclude that this consequence was within the realm of the defendant's intention.

This area of law has been subject to significant debate and development over the past few decades, there is a clear chronology of cases where the appeal courts have sought to establish a definitive test to determine where indirect intention is proved. **R v Woollin (1998)** is the current authority, although this still remains subject to some debate, this is the authority that should be explained and applied in application questions in the exam.

Key Case
R v Woollin (1998)

Facts: The defendant lost his temper with his 3-month-old son, he threw him onto a hard surface where he suffered a fractured skull and died. The defendant was convicted of murder. As it was not suggested that the defendant had direct intent, the judge gave the following direction regarding intention at the trial; 'the defendant has the relevant intent if he realised by his actions that there was a 'substantial risk' that he would suffer serious harm.'

Outcome: Guilty of manslaughter, not murder.

Legal principle: The reference to 'substantial risk' was incorrect and the definition of indirect intention given in R v Nedrick (1986) was the model direction; a jury should be directed that they are not entitled to infer the necessary intention, unless they feel sure that death or serious bodily harm was a virtual certainty (barring some unforeseen intervention) as a result of the defendant's actions and that the defendant appreciated that such was the case."

This case essentially establishes a two-part test:

1 Was the outcome (the actus reus / criminal consequence) a virtually certain consequence of the defendant's actions?

This is an objective test, it means the jury should consider as a matter of fact, was the actus reus a virtually certain consequence of the defendant's actions.

2 Did the defendant realise this?

This question introduces a subjective element into the test, in order to prove that a defendant indirectly intended a consequence it must be proved that the defendant themselves actually foresaw the criminal consequence as a 'virtually certainty'.

> **Example: Iona's Protest**
> Iona wanted to protest against the use of animals in medical testing, which took place at a nearby facility. To gain media attention for her protest she decided to break in and place a number of explosive devices inside the facility. When she later detonated them, several members of staff working at the facility were seriously injured. Whilst injury of the staff members was not Iona's direct intent (gaining media coverage was), a court may conclude that she indirectly intended such injury, as it is virtually certain that staff in close proximity would be injured if the explosive devices were detonated during work hours. Further, her knowledge of the facility would mean that she is likely to know this.

> **Exam Gold** When applying a defendant's mens rea, the most effective application not only cites the relevant facts from a scenario, but expands upon how those facts support that type of mens rea. For example, a scenario may say a defendant repeatedly hit the victim with an iron bar over the head, whilst they were in a fight, and continued when the victim was unconscious on the floor. Rather than just citing these facts from the scenario as evidence of possible direct intent to do serious harm (s18 GBH), a high-marking answer would emphasise the following:
>
> 1 The word 'repeatedly' means that the attack was sustained and the D wanted to continue until he was sure he had caused the desire harm
> 2 The use of a weapon demonstrates a desire to maximise the harm caused.
> 3 The head is a vulnerable area of the body well known to cause serious injury where harmed
> 4 The fact that the defendant continued the attack when the victim was defenceless on the floor suggests direct intent to cause serious harm as he chose to continue the attack when he was in no danger of harm himself.

Recklessness

Less serious offences will often require proof of either 'intention or recklessness' in relation to the actus reus of the offence. Recklessness is a less serious form of mens rea, a defendant is regarded as less culpable (blameworthy) where they commit an offence recklessly as opposed to intentionally.

Recklessness bares some similarity to the law of indirect intention, a defendant is reckless where they do not necessarily want the actus reus to occur, but there is a risk that it may occur as a consequence of their deliberate actions, and the defendant realised this and continued with their actions anyway, so that it is only fair to conclude that the defendant demonstrated a reckless mindset as to the actus reus occurring.

Key Case
R v Cunningham (1957)

Facts: The defendant went into the cellar of the empty house next door to his mother-in-laws and forcibly removed the gas meter from the wall. He tore it off the wall to get the money out of it and threw the meter away. The defendant did not turn off the gas linked to the meter and as a result, gas seeped through to next door where it was ingested by his mother-in-law whose life was endangered as a result. He was prosecuted for maliciously administering a noxious substance.

Outcome: Conviction quashed

Legal principle: Any reference to the word 'malice' within an offence indicates that either intention or recklessness is required, recklessness means that the defendant has foreseen the risk of the outcome occurring but nevertheless continued with his actions.

Recklessness has like the law of indirect intention been subject to debate in the common law, the courts disputing whether the law of recklessness should be objective or subjective. As it currently stands the case of **Cunningham (1957)** is the current authority, requiring subjective proof that the defendant foresaw the risk of the actus reus occurring in order to be regarded as having intended it. However, this has not always been the case since the decision in 1957, it was the case of **R v G (2003)** which re-instated the subjective test for recklessness from **Cunningham (1957)** as the required standard.

There is therefore a fine line between indirect intention and recklessness.

Indirect intention	v	Recklessness
D foresaw actus reus as a virtual certainty		D foresaw the risk the actus reus may occur

> **Exam Gold** In the exam, where you are discussing the mens rea of an offence which can be committed intentionally or recklessly, you should not explain and apply the principles of indirect intention. Indirect intention is a much higher and harder standard of foresight to prove, if the offence can be satisfied recklessly and the actus reus was not the defendant's direct intention you should explain and apply recklessness. You should therefore only explain and apply indirect intention in relation to offences that can only be committed intentionally, such as murder and s18 GBH / wounding, otherwise known as offences of specific intent.

Negligence

Within the context of mens rea in the criminal law it is essential to reference negligence. Negligence is technically not a type of mens rea, no offence references negligence within the mens rea, however, uniquely, the offence of gross negligence manslaughter does not require proof of either intention or recklessness, but rather evidence of fault via establishing negligence. Negligence is therefore a standard of fault that can be required in criminal offences.

The definition of negligence for this purpose is drawn from the civil law.

Blyth v Birmingham Waterworks (1856): "Negligence is the omission to do something which a reasonable man… would do, or doing something which a prudent and reasonable man would not do".

Negligence therefore establishes an objective standard of fault; fault is proved by comparing the defendant's actions to what would have been expected in those circumstances of the objective reasonable man. Any failure to adhere to those expected standards constitutes negligence.

> **Exam Gold** Many students find the application of mens rea the most challenging aspect of an application question. When applying mens rea you can discuss the defendant's motive (it is not the same as mens rea but can evidence it), what the circumstances of the incident suggest, any reference to the frame of mind of the defendant at the time of the offence, and other factors such as if it was pre-meditated or opportunistic, or if the defendant knew the victim etc.

Transferred malice

Whilst the law has developed definition of the different types of mens rea, there are also common law principles that can apply to all offences about how these types of mens rea will operate in particular circumstances. One such principle is the principle of transferred malice. Transferred malice is therefore not a type of mens rea but rather a principle of law about the operation of mens rea.

> **Exam Gold** If you are required to explain and apply the principle of transferred malice in the exam, you would still first have to discuss what type of mens rea the defendant had, to establish then that it could be transferred from one victim to another, in respect of the offence you are discussing.

The principle of transferred malice applies to cases where a defendant commits the actus reus of a criminal offence against a victim that was not their intended victim. The principle operates to move the mens rea from the intended victim (against which there was no actus reus) to the unintended victim (against whom the actus reus was in fact committed). The movement of the mens rea to the unintended victim means the defendant is therefore liable for an offence against the unintended victim. This principle is clearly founded upon fault and logic, it should be no defence to murder to say I shot the wrong person, where a defendant shoots and kills the wrong person. They have still caused the death of another intentionally; it just happens to be a different victim, other than the one they intended.

There are two circumstances where the principle of transferred malice operates.

1 Where the defendant commits the intended offence against an unintended victim, with no harm coming to the intended victim

This type of scenario may occur where a defendant aims to throw a heavy object and hit the defendant but misses and hits an innocent party stood nearby. The appropriate prosecution here is not an attempt as a full offence has been completed. In these circumstances the defendant has committed the actus reus against the unintended victim, and transferred malice transfers his mens rea from his intended to his unintended victim.

Key Case
R v Gnango (2011)

Facts: An innocent woman was crossing a car park whilst chatting on the phone and was shot in the head and killed. Two gunmen, the defendant and a rival unknown man referred to as 'Bandana Man' had been exchanging fire at each other across the carpark and she had been shot by mistake. Evidence showed that it was actually a shot from 'Bandana Man' that killed the victim, but under the principles of joint enterprise (outside of the A Level specification) the defendant was also guilty of causing her death and was convicted of murder.

Outcome: Guilty

Legal principle: D was clearly guilty of murder under operation of the principle of transferred malice, his malice of intention to kill moved from his intended victim (Bandana Man) to the unintended victim (the victim), whose death he actually caused.

2 Where an additional victim is harmed by the actions of the defendant

The second circumstance the principle of transferred malice can operate in involves circumstances where a defendant intends to commit an offence against their intended victim, and does so, but as a consequence of this act against the intended victim, accidentally harms a further unintended victim. In this situation the defendant has actus reus and mens rea against his intended victim, and the actus reus of an offence against the unintended victim. Transferred malice allows the mens rea to pass from the intended victim to the unintended victim, making the defendant guilty of an offence against both victims. The mens rea does not leave the intended victim, but rather moves in addition to the new additional victim.

Key Case
R v Mitchell (1983)

Facts: The defendant pushed an elderly gentleman in a post office queue, the elderly gentlemen (his intended victim) fell onto an elderly woman (his unintended victim), who subsequently died as a consequence of her injuries. The defendant was prosecuted for the offence of unlawful act manslaughter in relation to the elderly woman (his unintended victim).

Outcome: Guilty

Legal principle: The mens rea was transferred from his intended victim to the additional victim, making him guilty of an offence against the unintended additional victim.

Exam Gold Where you are explaining and applying the principle of transferred malice in an application question, make sure you clearly outline whether the defendant has just harmed the unintended victim, or if the unintended victim was harmed in addition to the intended victim. Your application should also explicitly state against which victims the defendant has actus reus / mens rea and be sure to clearly state how mens rea has moved from and to the victim.

Restrictions upon the operation of transferred malice

One way in which the operation of transferred malice is restricted, is that the mens rea can only transfer to complete the same offence as the defendant intended to commit. This means that if when attempting to commit an offence, the defendant not only misses their intended victim, but actually then goes on to commit a completely different type of offence, the mens rea cannot transfer to complete a different offence.

Key Case
Attorney General's Reference No. 3 of 1994

Facts: At around 22-24 weeks pregnant, the victim was stabbed multiple times by the defendant, the father of the unborn child. The defendant clearly had intention to cause grievous bodily harm to the mother. 17 days after the stabbing the victim went into early labour and whilst the baby was born alive, the baby died 121 days later as a consequence of the premature birth, caused by the defendant's actions. The defendant was prosecuted for the murder of the unborn child for which he was acquitted.

Outcome: No liability outcome – Attorney General's references involve reviewing points of law

Legal principle: The principle of transferred malice could not apply here as it only operates where the mens rea of one crime causes the actus reus of another crime. The mens rea of intent to seriously harm the mother, a living being, could not be transferred to intent to harm the foetus, a foetus not being legally recognised as a living person that is capable of being murdered.

Example: Transferred Malice

A defendant wishes to break the window of his local fish and chip shop. He wants to do so because he has an ongoing feud with the owner.	Late at night, when he believed no-one to be around, the defendant goes to the fish and chip shop with a brick and throws it with force at the window. **MR – intention to destroy or damage (criminal damage).**	The brick not only breaks the window, but hits one of the employees of the fish and chip shop who is working inside, after hours, cleaning out the fryers. **AR – battery occasioning actual bodily harm.**

In these circumstances, although the **mens** rea of criminal damage cannot transfer to complete the offence of battery occasioning actual bodily harm against the fish and chip shop employee, as there is not an offence that has this actus reus and mens rea combined. In order to establish liability in relation to the non-fatal offence, the prosecution would likely have to rely upon the mens rea of recklessness.

Strict liability

'Strict Liability' is not a type of mens rea, but a type of offence which requires no/partial mens rea in relation to some or all of the actus reus. These offences are often known as 'no fault' offences, proof of the criminalised act alone is sufficient to enforce liability, no fault in terms of foresight needs to be proven. State of affairs offences (chapter 1) are a form of strict liability offences.

It is important to note if reading around this area, that there is a distinction between strict liability offences and absolute liability offences. As described a strict liability offence requires no/partial mens rea in relation to some of the actus reus, an absolute offence requires no mens rea in relation to any of the elements of actus reus.

Strict liability offences are normally 'regulatory' and not regarded as crimes committed by criminals e.g., speeding, health and safety regulations and various pollution offences. As a consequence, strict liability offences often attract minor sentences, such as fines, as these can be enforced against companies and corporations. Strict liability offences are normally created by Parliament and defined in a statute.

Just because a statute makes no reference to mens rea does not automatically mean that the offence is one of strict liability. The courts always start with the presumption that the offence is one that does require mens rea and will only displace this presumption where it can be proved that the crime is one of social concern and it is necessary to impose strict liability because this will protect the public by enforcing higher standards within the community.

Key Case
Sweet v Parsley (1970)

Facts: The defendant rented her property to tenants, during their tenancy drugs were found within the property and the defendant was prosecuted for being concerned in the management of premises being used for the purpose of smoking cannabis resin. The defendant denied liability upon the basis that she had no awareness that the illegal activity was happening. The question for the court was whether this was a strict liability offence, as the statute appeared to suggest, if so, her lack of knowledge was irrelevant.

Outcome: Not guilty

Legal principle: Where there is dispute about the nature of the offence, the courts should first consider the wording of the act, even where there is no indication of mens rea, the presumption is still that Parliament intended for mens rea to be required. In order to determine the true nature of the offence, the courts should look outside of the Act to determine the intention of Parliament and if Parliament intended to create a strict liability offence this must be enforced. A quasi-criminal offence is more likely to be a strict liability offence. This offence did require mens rea despite no explicit reference to it within the statute.

Key Case
R v Williams (2001)

Facts: The defendant regularly drove a car, despite the fact that he had neither a driving licence nor insurance. The defendant was driving along a dual carriageway, adhering to the speed limit, when the victim stepped out in front of his car, the defendant could not avoid hitting him and the victim died as a result of the injuries sustained. The Crown accepted that there was no fault or carelessness in the defendant's driving, but he was nevertheless prosecuted for 'causing death by driving when unlicensed, disqualified or uninsured.' The defence argued that the offence required some fault to be proved, as in these circumstances a licensed insured driver would face no penalty as the standard of driving was not at fault.

Outcome: Guilty

Legal principle: Whilst generally criminal offences require proof of an Act alongside fault or blameworthiness, the wording of the statute here is clear, liability can be imposed without any proof of fault or blameworthy conduct. This was the offence that was created by Parliament.

Reasons for strict liability offences

1. **Strict liability offences save the legal system time and money:** strict liability offences do not require lengthy prosecutions or court time. For most offences the defendant will be notified in writing and simply pay a fine as their punishment, for example when a person is caught speeding, they get notification through the post of the offence and a date by which to make payment. There is little cost associated with this process. This therefore means that organisations such as the courts and the probation service are not required, and a substantial amount of money is saved. The courts can therefore be saved for offences which require discussion in court.

2. **Strict liability offences act as a deterrent:** in areas where strict liability offences are enforced, this acts as a deterrent to potential offenders as they know, if they are caught, they will be convicted whatever the circumstances. This lack of opportunity to defend liability is hoped to deter individuals from undertaking those acts.

3. **Strict liability offences place the onus on individuals to be responsible for their actions:** where an offence is one of strict liability, this encourages potential defendants to undertake higher standards of care in fear of conviction for an offence. The onus on maintaining standards and not undertaking criminal actions is placed on defendants as they know that they will have no defence if they have committed a strict liability offence.

4. **Strict liability offences are quasi-criminal offences:** whilst many argue that the existence of such offences is unfair, strict liability offences only tend to be minor in nature, so a strict liability conviction is unlikely to have a significantly detrimental effect on an individual. For example, individuals who are caught speeding for the first time tend to get a £100 and 3 penalty points.

Coincidence of actus reus and mens rea

Like the principle of transferred malice, **coincidence** of actus reus and mens rea is not a type of mens rea that can satisfy an offence, but rather a principle regarding how the mens rea of an offence can apply, specifically regarding when it is proved in relation to the actus reus. The coincidence principle is also commonly referred to as the **'contemporaneity principle'**.

According to this principle, it is a general principle of criminal liability, that the actus reus and mens rea of an offence must be present at the same time, they must coincide. In other words, the defendant must have had the guilty mind when he was carrying out the guilty act. If the two are not present simultaneously a defendant will not be guilty of an offence.

Interestingly, the courts have been presented with a number of cases where there is technically no coincidence of actus reus and mens rea, but the defendant has clearly demonstrated fault and should be found guilty of the offence. The courts have modified the generic principle to enable liability to be imposed in these cases. Two modifications to the principle have been developed, the continuing act principle and the single transaction principle.

1 The continuing act principle

In some cases, the defendant may commit the actus reus of an offence without realising, upon realisation they then chose to continue the actus reus. In order to prevent a defendant claiming that the actus reus was complete before the mens rea began (and thus avoiding liability), the courts have developed the continuing act principle.

According to this principle, the actus reus of a crime is not complete when it is undertaken, but rather can continue throughout a whole chain of events and provided that mens rea can be established at some point during this continuing actus reus, there is sufficient coincidence of actus reus and mens rea.

> **Key Case**
> **Fagan v Metropolitan Police Commissioner (1968)**
>
> **Facts:** The defendant was driving when a police officer indicated that he should pull over, when the defendant did so the officer indicated that he was not close enough to the kerb and asked him to move closer, when the defendant did so, he, in error parked the car on the officer's foot. When the police officer asked him to move, he refused and switched the engine off, but eventually did reverse the car to remove it from the officer's foot. The defence claimed there was no offence as the actus reus was complete before the mens rea was evident.
>
> **Outcome:** Guilty
>
> **Legal principle:** Actus reus can continue throughout an action, there is no requirement that the mens rea is also present at the start of the actus reus, it is enough that the mens rea is evident at some point in the sense that it is superimposed.

2 The single transaction principle

In some cases, there may not be coincidence of actus reus and mens rea, but the continuing act principle cannot be relied upon because the guilty act does not occur until later in the chain of events, well after the mens rea was present. In order to ensure liability for blameworthy offenders in circumstances such as this the courts have developed the single transaction principle.

According to the single transaction principle, a series of connected act can be regarded as one single transaction for the purposes of coincidence of actus reus and mens rea, and provided that actus reus and mens rea is evident within this, there is sufficient coincidence.

Key Case
R v Thabo Meli (1954)

Facts: Four men planned to murder the victim at a hut, and then fake an accident to hide their criminal acts. The four men brought the victim to the hut, and he was hit around the back of the head with a heavy metal object. The blow to the head caused him to lose consciousness, but the defendants believed him to be deceased, and subsequently rolled him over a low cliff and arranged the scene to appear like he had an accident. The post-mortem revealed that the defendant was not killed by the blow to the head, but rather exposure whilst on the cliff. The defence claimed they could not be guilty of murder as they had no mens rea when the death was caused (on the cliff) because they believed him already to be dead, there were two separate acts where the actus reus and mens rea were separate.

Outcome: Guilty

Legal principle: It is not always appropriate to divide up what can be regarded as one series of acts, provided that actus reus and mens rea is proved within this series of acts, this is sufficient to prove liability, it is no defence to say they believed their guilty act was completed before it in fact was.

Example: Coincidence

Alice is learning to become a flame-thrower, and despite her flatmates telling her not to practice inside, she does so.

Alice puts her extinguished flame throwers on her bed, before going for a shower. They are still extremely hot and start a fire without her realising.

AR – destruction or damage by fire (arson).

Alice gets out the shower and is horrified to find the fire, she decides to make it look like an accident, rather than admitting her mistake, so deliberately leaves the lit flame throwers there causing a fire, whilst not notifying the emergency services.

MR – intention to destroy or damage by fire (arson).

In these circumstances although Alice had no mens rea when the fire initially began, she had mens rea when she deliberately chose to leave the existing fire in her room. In this situation she may deny liability upon the basis that the actus reus was complete when the fire had started, and she had no mens rea at this point. The courts would apply the continuing act principle and say that the actus reus continued throughout the whole time the fire was active, her mens rea of deliberately choosing to leave the fire, purposeful of covering up her accident, was sufficient coincidence.

> **Exam Gold** In an application question, where it appears that there is some issue with coincidence, you should recognise this and begin by explaining the generic principle. You should then identify where in the scenario you believe the actus reus and mens rea to be present and apply the relevant principle accordingly (continuing act or single transaction).
>
> Where the mens rea occurs later during an ongoing act that constitutes the actus reus, this indicates you should apply the continuing act principle. Where there is mens rea at first, but actus reus completed later, this may indicate that you should be discussing the single transaction principle.

Key Terms – General Elements of Liability: Mens Rea

Mens rea	The mental element of a criminal offence, as specified within the definition of the crime that must be proved alongside the actus reus.
Motive	The reasons why the defendant committed the criminal offence, entirely distinct to mens rea, but may be relevant to the availability of defences and sentencing.
Objective	A test that considers the foresight of a reasonable person rather than the particular defendant.
Subjective	A test that considers the foresight of the particular defendant rather than what the reasonable person would have foreseen in those circumstances.
Intention	A type of mens rea that can be required by a criminal offence, either direct or indirect, which reflects the highest level of fault.
Direct intention	A defendant has direct intention where they have decided they want to carry out the actus reus of a criminal offence.
Indirect intention	A defendant indirectly intends the actus reus of a criminal offence, where although it is not what they have set out to achieve, they realise that it will happen as a virtually certain consequence of their actions and continue with them anyway.
Recklessness	A defendant is reckless as to the actus reus of an offence occurring, where they realise there is a risk it may occur as a consequence of their actions, and chose to take that risk. Recklessness is a subjective test.
Negligence	This is a standard of fault which is required to be proved within the offence of gross negligence manslaughter instead of the traditional mens rea of either intention or recklessness, the definition is drawn from the common law.
Transferred malice	A principle of mens rea that allows a defendant's mens rea to move from an intended victim to unintended victim, making them guilty of a complete offence against an unintended victim.
Strict liability	A type of offence which requires no/partial mens rea in relation to some or all of the actus reus.
Coincidence of actus reus and mens rea	A general principle of criminal liability that requires the actus reus and mens rea of a criminal offence to be present at the same time.
Continuing act principle	A principle recognising that is some cases the actus reus of an offence continues throughout an action, in order for coincidence of actus reus and mens rea to be proved it does not have to be established that the mens rea is evidence throughout the whole of the actus reus, provided it is evident at some point.
The single transaction principle	A principle recognising that sometimes it is not appropriate to divide a series of actions up into separate actions, where there is one series of connected acts it is sufficient for the principle of coincidence that actus reus and mens rea is evident within the chain of events.

One Sentence Case Summary – General Elements of Liability: Mens Reus

Name	Topic Link	Legal significance
R v Inglis (2011)	**Mens rea – motive**	Where all the elements of an offence are present, the motive of a defendant does not render these elements unproved, here a mercy killing still demonstrated intention to kill.
R v Mohan (1976)	**Mens rea – direct intention**	Direct intention is the 'decision to bring about the criminal consequence'.

One Sentence Case Summary – General Elements of Liability: Mens Reus

Name	Topic Link	Legal significance
R v Woollin (1998)	Mens rea – indirect intention	The model direction for indirect (oblique) intention is to be drawn from the case of Nedrick, 'a jury should be directed that they are not entitled to infer the necessary intention, unless they feel sure that death or serious bodily harm was a virtual certainty (barring some unforeseen intervention) as a result of the defendant's actions and that the defendant appreciated that such was the case.
R v Cunningham (1957)	Mens rea – recklessness	The word 'maliciously' does not require proof of wickedness but rather intention or recklessness, recklessness means the defendant foresaw the risk of the outcome occurring but continued with his acts anyway.
Blyth v Birmingham Waterworks (1856)	Mens rea – negligence	"Negligence is the omission to do something which a reasonable man, guided upon those considerations that ordinarily regulate human affairs, would do, or doing something which a prudent and reasonable man would not do".
R v Gnango (2011)	Mens rea – transferred malice	Where a defendant commits a criminal offence against an unintended victim, the malice (mens rea) transfers to the unintended victim making them guilty of an offence against that unintended victim.
R v Mitchell (1983)	Mens rea – transferred malice	Where a defendant commits a criminal offence against their intended victim, but also causes harm to an unintended victim, the mens rea for the intended victim can transfer to the unintended victim in addition, making the defendant guilty of an offence against both victims.
Attorney General's Reference No. 3 of 1994	Mens rea – transferred malice	The mens rea of one crime cannot transfer to the actus reus of a different offence.
Sweet v Parsley (1970)	Mens rea – strict liability	Where an offence has no explicit reference to mens rea this does not automatically mean the offence is one of strict liability, the presumption is still that Parliament intended for mens rea to be required.
R v Williams (2011)	Mens rea – strict liability	Where the wording and intention of Parliament is clear, a strict liability offence must be enforced without the need to prove fault or blame on behalf of the defendant.
Fagan v Metropolitan Police Commissioner (1968)	Mens rea – continuing act principle	When determining if there is sufficient coincidence of actus reus and mens rea, the continuing act principle can apply, this means the actus reus of a crime can continue throughout an action, there is no requirement that the mens rea is also present at the start of the actus reus, it is enough that the mens rea is evident at some point.
R v Thabo Meli (1954)	Mens rea – single transaction principle	When establishing coincidence of actus reus and mens rea it is not always necessary to divide up what can be regarded as one series of acts, provided that actus reus and mens rea is proved within this series of acts this is sufficient to prove liability, it is no defence to say they believed their guilty act was completed before it in fact was.

FATAL OFFENCES AGAINST THE PERSON - MURDER

Exam Reference:	H418/01 – The Legal System and Criminal Law (Paper 1)
	Murder is a substantive topic that appears in paper 1 of the OCR Law A-Level exam series. 60 marks out of 80 are allocated to substantive law topics in this paper. You will be required to accurately identify and explain (AO1) and then apply (AO2) the law on murder to scenario facts.
Topic Content:	• Common law offence of murder

Murder

Murder is a homicide offence; this means that the actus reus involves the killing of one human being by another. It is important to remember that just because a defendant has caused the death of a victim, they are not automatically guilty of murder, there are also the manslaughter offences, or death may have been accidental and not criminal (unlawful).

Despite being one of the most serious criminal offences, murder has never been criminalised by statute, the definition currently used in the courts was provided by Lord Coke in the 17th Century.

'… the unlawful killing of a reasonable creature in being, and under the King (or Queens) peace, with malice aforethought, express or implied.'

Whilst this definition may appear old and out of date, in practice it works well and is a functional definition used within the criminal courts.

Elements of the offence

Actus reus	Mens rea
1 **Unlawful killing**, the defendant has caused the death of the victim.	**Malice aforethought**, express or implied.
2 The victim is a **reasonable creature** in being.	
3 The act was committed under the **Queens peace**.	

Murder is one of few offences that carries a mandatory sentence, this means that a judge does not have discretion in the type of sentence that is imposed on the defendant is found or pleads guilty, they must enforce a life sentence. A life sentence does not actually mean life in prison, a prison sentence of the rest of the defendant's life is known as a 'whole life order' and only reserved for the most serious of cases, of which can be murder. Whole life orders are reserved for cases that involve circumstances reflecting a high level of seriousness *e.g., if it involved the killing and abduction of a child*. A life sentence imposed upon conviction of murder means that a defendant is subject to a criminal sentence for the rest of their life, but not all of this is spent in prison. When imposing a life sentence a judge will specify a 'tariff', this is the minimum number of years that the offender will spend in prison before they submit an application for parole (release), which is not guaranteed. When released the offender remains on licence and can be re-called to prison at any time, for the protection of themselves or others. The tariff imposed on the offender will vary according to the circumstances of the case (see examples below).

Statutory reference: Schedule 21 Sentencing Act 2020

S3(2)
- **a** in the case of an offence committed before 13 April 2015, the murder of a police officer or prison officer in the course of his or her duty,
- **b** a murder involving the use of a firearm or explosive,
- **c** a murder done for gain such as a murder done in the course or furtherance of robbery or burglary, done for payment or done in the expectation of gain as a result of the death,
- **d** a murder intended to obstruct or interfere with the course of justice,
- **e** a murder involving sexual or sadistic conduct,

> **Statutory reference: Schedule 21 Sentencing Act 2020**
>
>   **f** the murder of two or more persons,
>
>   **g** a murder that is aggravated by racial or religious hostility or by hostility related to sexual orientation,
>
>   **h** a murder that is aggravated by hostility related to disability or transgender identity, where the offence was committed on or after 3 December 2012 (or over a period, or at some time during a period, ending on or after that date
>
> For the above circumstances the starting point for the minimum tariff is 30 years.

⭐ **Exam Gold** Whilst it is good practice to be aware of the maximum sentences for each criminal offence, in an application question it is not required to include the maximum sentence for a crime. You can however, use the sentencing powers for murder, when discussing the topic of sentencing within section A of Paper 1.

Actus reus

1 Unlawful killing

The first element of the murder offence requires proof that the defendant unlawfully killed the victim.

The word unlawful means that the defendant has no available defence to them, or that the killing was not lawful for any other reason e.g., death caused by a firearms officer in lawful execution of their duty. If there does appear to be a relevant defence in the exam, discuss this after you completed your discussion of the offence.

The word killing means that it must be established that the defendant caused the death of the victim, the definition does not specify the way that the death must have been caused (this is likely impossible as there are so many ways this could be achieved) but rather what is criminalised within the actus is the causing of death where there is no lawful excuse.

Murder is a therefore a result crime, and both areas of factual and legal causation must be proved. There are no special causation principles for murder, the standard common law principles to establish causation in fact and in law apply *(discussed in chapter 1)*. In accordance with the principles of legal causation, for murder it therefore does not need to be proved that the defendant is the only or main cause of death, but that they were an operating cause of the death.

It is important to note that the definition of murder does not require an 'act causing the death', rather it requires a 'killing', this means a defendant may commit the offence of murder by **omission,** it is however important to remember that in accordance with the generic omission principles, an offence can only be committed by omission where the defendant is under a duty to act.

> ### Key Case
> ### R v Gibbins and Proctor (1918)
>
> **Facts:** Gibbin's wife had left him, so him and his daughter Nelly, aged 7 years, went to live with another woman, Proctor. The family had sufficient funds to support all residing within the house, but Nelly was deliberately starved which caused her death. The defendants then hid the child's body and buried it in a brickyard in order to conceal her death. The two defendants were charged with her murder.
>
> **Outcome:** Guilty.
>
> **Legal principle:** The defendants were guilty of murder by omission, the father was under a duty to act based upon the familial relationship, Proctor was also acting as a parent as in reality she was undertaken the role of the child's mother.

It is however important to note that the offence of unlawful act (constructive) manslaughter can also be committed by omission, so death caused via a failure to act does not automatically indicate a murder.

As quoted by Lord Mustill in **Airedale National Health Trust v Bland (1993)** "… a person may be criminally liable for the consequences of an omission if he stands in such relation to the victim that he is under a duty to act. Where the result is death, the offence will usually be manslaughter, but if the necessary intent is proved it will be murder".

> **Example: Underlying Conditions**
> Harry attacks Mickey with a machete, killing him. Following the post-mortem examination, it was discovered that Mickey had terminal cancer and in fact had very little time left to live at the time of the attack. This would not prevent Harry from being guilty of murder, he was the cause of death at that moment.

2 Reasonable creature in being

It must be proved that the victim was a 'reasonable creature in being' at the time of the defendant's act causing death. This generally means that they are a living human being. It is not possible to commit the offence of murder in relation to a human that is already deceased, an inanimate object or even animal.

There are two states of the human form where there has been debate surrounding the status of 'reasonable creature in being'.

a **Foetus:** a foetus is an unborn child within the womb of their mother. A foetus is not a reasonable creature in being. This is because to recognise a foetus as a reasonable creature in being would grant it lawful rights within the criminal law which would have significant implications for procedures of lawful abortion.

Where a defendant does cause the 'death' of a foetus capable of being born alive they may be guilty of the offence of child destruction under the **Infant Life (Preservation) Act 1929,** although this sits outside of the OCR syllabus.

The question then arises, at what point does a foetus become a reasonable creature in being? The general principle of law is that it is a reasonable creature in being when fully expelled from the mother.

In the case of **Rance v Mid-Downs Health Authority (1991)** it was held that a child is born alive if it is 'and living by reason of its breathing through its own lungs alone, without deriving any of its living or power of living by or through any connection with it's mother.'

> ### Key Case
> ### Attorney General's Reference No. 3 of 1994 (1997)
>
> **Facts:** At around 22-24 weeks pregnant, the victim was stabbed multiple times by the defendant, the father of the unborn child. The defendant clearly had intention to cause grievous bodily harm to the mother. 17 days after the stabbing the victim went into early labour and whilst the baby was born alive, the baby died 121 days later as a consequence of the premature birth, caused by the defendant's actions. The defendant was prosecuted for the murder of the unborn child for which he was acquitted.
>
> **Outcome:** No liability outcome – Attorney General's references involve reviewing points of law
>
> **Legal principle:** It has been established beyond doubt in the criminal law that foetus has no recognition as a reasonable creature in being. In these circumstances however, it may be possible to convict a defendant of unlawful act manslaughter, provided it could be foreseen by the reasonable man that the act be dangerous toward the unborn child after birth, and the principles of causation be proven.

b **Brain-dead**

Another state of the human form that has raised debate in this area is where a victim is medically recognised as brain-dead. This discussion has often arisen in cases where causation is in dispute, and a defendant who has attacked a victim is seeking to prove that the doctor who turned off the life-support machine / withdrew life-sustaining treatment is in fact the case of death.

Key Case
R v Malcherek & Steel (1981)

Facts: This case concerned two appeals on similar facts. Both defendants had been convicted of murder following the carrying out of attacks on their victims who were later found upon medical diagnosis to be brain-dead, the decision was therefore made by medical staff to discontinue life support treatment via the switching off of machines. In both trials the issue of causation was not left to the jury to determine. Both appeals contended that the judge should have left the issue of causation to the jury, to determine if the actions of the doctors in turning off the life support machines were in fact the cause of death.

Outcome: Guilty

Legal principle: Whilst the case was not deciding this point of law, it recognised that medical opinion supports recognition of death in the 'irreversible death of the brain-stem', despite the fact that a bodies functions e.g., breathing can be continued past this point with medical support.

Exam Gold In an application question, if the elements of reasonable creature in being and under the Queen's peace are not in dispute, simply mention them and recognise them as satisfied. You do not need to spend significant time explaining these principles if not in dispute.

3 Under the Queens peace
Under the Queens peace refers to whether the killing took place in the course of war, if it did not, then it can amount to murder.

Mens rea: Malice aforethought, express or implied

Within Lord Coke's common law definition of murder, the phrase that makes reference to the mens rea of the defendant is **'malice aforethought, express or implied'**. The modern understanding of the mens rea of murder demonstrates that these words now mean little in relation to what will actually satisfy the mens rea of murder.

In **Attorney Generals reference (No 3 of 1994) (1997)** Lord Mustill is quoted as saying 'the law of homicide is permeated by anomaly, fiction, misnomer and obsolete reasoning. One conspicuous anomaly is the rule which identifies the "malice aforethought" (a doubly misleading expression) required for the crime of murder not only with a conscious intention to kill but also with an intention to cause grievous bodily harm. It is, therefore, possible to commit a murder not only without wishing the death of the victim but without the least thought that this might be the result of the assault'.

As indicated by Lord Mustill, within the mens rea of murder there is no need to prove 'malice' from the defendant to victim, further there is no need to prove 'aforethought' in relation to the death or the acts that caused the death, the killing does not need to be pre-meditated or specifically need to be proven as 'malicious'.

The modern interpretation of the mens rea of murder is:

Express malice aforethought: intention to kill.

Implied malice aforethought: intention to do grievous bodily harm.

Only one of the above needs to be proved. In accordance with implied malice aforethought, a defendant can be convicted of murder with no intention or foresight of death.

It is also important to note that the offence of murder cannot be committed recklessly. Therefore, the principles of indirect intention are extremely important here as the lowest form of mens rea that will satisfy the offence of murder is 'indirect intentioncause grievous bodily harm'. There is a fine line between this and the mens rea that can satisfy the offence of unlawful act manslaughter.

One area of mens rea within the context of murder that is often of academic interest is euthanasia. assisted suicide. Euthanasia is the deliberate ending of another person's life in order to end the suffering they are experiencing, usual due to chronic or terminal illness. Assisted suicide is where a person aids another in the ending of their own life. Despite multiple campaigns to legalise both, both euthanasia and assisted suicide remain illegal under the criminal law. Assisted suicide is a criminal offence under the **Suicide Act 1961** and has a maximum sentence of 14 years imprisonment. Euthanasia (also known as a mercy killing) may be regarded as murder.

Key Case
R v Inglis (2011)

Facts: Following an accident, a young man suffered catastrophic head injuries, his mother unsuccessfully attempted to kill her son with a lethal dose of heroin. One year later, she tried again and was successful in her attempt resulting in the death of her son, motivated by a desire to wish to relieve his suffering, and prevent a painful death following the withdrawal of life support. She was convicted of both attempted murder and murder.

Outcome: Guilty

Legal principle: The law or murder does not distinguish between defendants who intend to kill out of love or intend to kill out of malice. Whilst motivated by mercy, a mercy killing does not negate the requirements of murder. Motive does not counteract the presence of all elements of the offence.

Exam Gold Murder may arise in an application question with a potential defence present. This could be either of the partial defences i.e., loss of control or diminished responsibility, but also any of the general defences i.e., intoxication / insanity / automatism / self-defence / duress.

Key Terms – Fatal Offences Against the Person - Murder	
Homicide	The killing of one human being by another.
Murder	A criminal offence whereby the defendant unlawfully kills a reasonably creature in being, under the Queens peace, with intention to kill or cause grievous bodily harm.
Mandatory life sentence	The sentence that must be imposed upon a finding of murder.
Minimum tariff	The minimum amount of time that a defendant convicted of murder will be in prison, before they can apply for parole.
Unlawful killing	The actus reus of murder requires proof that the defendant, without lawful excuse caused the death of the victim.
Reasonable creature in being	At the time of the act that caused death it must be proved that the defendant is a reasonable creature in being.
Foetus	An unborn child, within the womb of it's mother that is not a reasonable creature in being.
Under the Queens peace	A killing will amount to murder provided it occurs outside the course of war.
Malice aforethought	The mens rea of murder, which can be expressed or implied.
Express malice aforethought	Intention to kill (direct or indirect).
Implied malice aforethought	Intention (direct of indirect) to cause the victim grievous bodily harm.
Euthanasia/mercy killing	Deliberately ending the life of another in order to put a stop to their pain and suffering.
Assisted suicide	Aiding another in committing suicide.

One Sentence Case Summary – Fatal Offences Against the Person - Murder		
Name	**Topic Link**	**Legal significance**
R v Gibbins and Proctor (1918)	Murder - omission	If a parent, or stepparent acting as 'loco parentis' fails to adequately care and provide for a child and this causes the death of the child with the intent to kill or cause GBH, they are under a duty to act and their failure to act can amount to the actus reus of murder.
Airedale National Health Trust v Bland (1993)	Murder – omission	Where the necessary intent is proved and the defendant is under a duty to act, the offence of murder can be committed by omission.
Rance v Mid-Downs Health Authority (1991)	Murder – reasonable creature in being	A foetus only becomes a reasonable creature in being when breathing through its own lungs and no longer living through any connection with its mother.
Attorney General's Reference No. 3 of 1994 (1997)	Murder – reasonable creature in being	Where a foetus in injured in the womb via an attack on the mother and born alive, but later dies as a result of the initial attack, this cannot be grounds for murder, but a defendant may be guilty of unlawful act manslaughter in relation to the baby provided its elements are proved.
R v Malcherek & Steel (1981)	Murder – reasonable creature in being	Whilst the case was not deciding this point of law, it recognised that medical opinion supports recognition of death in the 'irreversible death of the brain-stem', despite the fact that a bodies functions e.g., breathing can be continued past this point with medical support.
Attorney General's Reference No. 3 of 1994 (1997)	Murder – malice aforethought	The phrase 'malice aforethought' is a 'doubly misleading expression', it is in fact possible to have the mens rea of murder without any foresight of death at all.
R v Inglis (2011)	Murder – malice aforethought – mercy killings	Whilst motivated by mercy, a mercy killing does not negate the requirements of murder, an intent to kill is nevertheless an intent to kill, even if motivated by mercy.

FATAL OFFENCES AGAINST THE PERSON – VOLUNTARY MANSLAUGHTER

Exam Reference:	H418/01 – The Legal System and Criminal Law (Paper 1)
	Voluntary manslaughter covers the topics of diminished responsibility and loss of control which are substantive topics that appear in paper 1 of the OCR Law A-Level exam series. 60 marks out of 80 are allocated to substantive law topics in this paper. You will be required to accurately identify and explain (AO1) and apply (AO2) the tests for voluntary manslaughter to scenario facts.
Topic Content:	• Loss of control (s54 Coroners and Justice Act 2009)
	• Diminished responsibility (s2 Homicide Act 1957 as amended by s52 Coroners and Justice Act 2009)

Topic overview

Voluntary manslaughter is a topic that sits within the law of homicide, where one human being kills another. Voluntary manslaughter is however, not an offence that a defendant can be charged with, it is rather a partial **defences** which forms a type of manslaughter that a defendant can be convicted of and a verdict that can be delivered, where they have been prosecuted for murder but have been able to rely upon a partial defence. A partial defence is one that does not result in an acquittal but reduces the conviction of a defendant.

Where a defendant is prosecuted for murder, but they successfully plead either diminished responsibility or loss of control, they will not be found guilty of murder, but rather convicted of voluntary manslaughter. This has significant implications for sentencing, as voluntary manslaughter does not carry the mandatory life sentence that murder does, but instead has a discretionary life maximum sentence where the judge has options.

It is important to note that successfully pleading a partial defence is not a denial of murder, rather inadvertently it is an admission of causing the death of the victim with the required mens rea, the defence is rather a claim that there were justifiable mitigating circumstances surrounding commission of the murder that justify a reduction in the conviction.

There is a third partial defence; killing in pursuance of a suicide pact (s59 Coroners and Justice Act 2009), but this is not covered within the OCR syllabus. Infanticide (s57 Coroners and Justice Act 2009) is also a relevant defence to a murder conviction, but again not covered within the OCR syllabus.

Loss of control and diminished responsibility are both special defences, this means that they are only available to a charge of murder and cannot be used in relation to any other offence.

Two defences, provocation and diminished responsibility were first introduced in the **Homicide Act 1957**, when the death penalty was still available for a conviction of murder. The area of law was radically reformed in the **Coroners and Justice Act 2009**. The defence of diminished responsibility was updated, and the former defence of provocation was abolished and the defence of loss of control was established.

The provisions of the **Coroners and Justice Act 2009** came into force on 4th October 2010, any prosecution for murders that took place before that date have to be tried in accordance with the law of that date, namely the defence of provocation or the unamended defence of diminished responsibility.

> **Exam Gold** In an application question you do not need to refer to the historical context of either defence. Application questions rather require you to explain and apply the up-to-date law.

Loss of control

Loss of control is a statutory defence that was created by and is contained in s54 of the **Coroners and Justice Act 2009**. The same statute abolished the law of provocation under s56 – *'(1) The common law defence of provocation is abolished and replaced by sections 54 and 55'*.

When the new loss of control defence was introduced, replacing the previous defence of provocation, there was clear emphasis that this statute was new and in no way linked to the previous defence of provocation. In the case of **R v Clinton, Parker & Evans (2012)** the Lord Chief Justice stated '… the new statutory defence is self-contained. Its common law heritage is irrelevant.' This statement clearly outlines that there should be no reliance upon common law authorities from before the **Coroners and Justice Act 2009**, these cases are now irrelevant and no longer act as authorities. The defence of loss of control is new and independent of the defence of provocation, despite the fact that there are many similarities between the two.

There are three elements of the defence outlined in the statute, all elements must be proved in order for the defence to be available.

The test for loss of control

1 The defendant's acts / omissions resulted from the defendant's **loss of self-control**;
2 The loss of self-control **resulted from a qualifying trigger**, and;
3 A person of the **defendant's sex and age, with a normal degree of tolerance and self-restraint and in the circumstances of the defendant**, might have reacted in the **same or in a similar way to the defendant**.

1 **Loss of control**
s54(a) D's acts or omissions in doing or being party to the killing resulted from D's loss of control.

In accordance with this element, it must be proven that the defendant lost control at the time that they carried out the acts or omissions which caused the death of the victim. No further definition of what a loss of control is, is contained within the statue. This therefore suggests that this is a question of fact to be determined by the jury within the trial.

Key Case
R v Jewell (2014)

Facts: The defendant and victim worked together, and the defendant would as a matter of agreement, collect the victim for work in the morning. One morning when collecting the victim, the defendant got out of his van and shot the victim twice in the stomach killing him. When apprehended by police later the same day, the defendant was found to have a gun, ammunition, knives and a number of other items. The defendant denied intending to kill but instead said he had 'snapped', that it was like there was an injection or explosion in his head as a result of intimidation leading up to the event, believing the victim to be one of the perpetrators. Whilst the defendant denied a premeditated murder, he had stolen the van the night before and made arrangements for his cat so he could leave immediately the next day, which he attempted to do. The judge ruled that there was insufficient evidence to raise the defence of loss of control.

Outcome: Defence of loss of control not allowed

Legal principle: A judge does not have to leave the defence of loss of control to the jury where they believe that no jury could properly conclude there is a basis for the defence. Further, whilst there is no definition of loss of control within the statute, an appropriate academic definition that can be followed is '… a loss of the ability to act in accordance with considered judgment or a loss of normal powers of reasoning'.

Whilst the statute does not define what a loss of control is, it does provide further clarification upon other aspects of the loss of control requirement.

Exam Gold In practice, determining whether the defendant has lost control is a question of fact to be determined by the jury, this means in an exam question you should speculate upon whether the defendant has lost control by discussing any relevant facts that you have available.

s54(2) ... it does not matter whether the loss of control is sudden.

Within the statute it clearly establishes that there is no requirement the loss of control be a sudden reaction to the qualifying trigger advanced. The act however does not establish a timeline, or time-limit about the extent of the time that is allowed to pass between the qualifying trigger and the loss of control for the defence to still be available. Interpretations of the courts since the introduction of that Act seem to clarify that whilst a delay does not prevent the defence being available, the longer the delay, the less likely it is that there was a loss of control.

It is important to remember that whilst a delay is acceptable, it still must be proved that the delay was in response to the qualifying trigger, if this is not proven, the defence will not be available.

This provision means that if the defendant has a 'slow burn' reaction, a reaction a significant amount of time after the qualifying trigger(s), the defence may still be available; this can be common in women suffering from 'battered woman syndrome'.

> **Key Case**
> ### R v Dawes, Hatter and Bowyer (2013)
>
> **Facts:** This case involved the combined appeals of three defendants against their convictions for murder. All three defendants appealed upon the basis that there were errors of law in the dismissal or application of loss of control within their cases.
>
> **Outcome:** Appeals dismissed
>
> **Legal principle:** A reaction may be delayed, this reflects the fact that all individuals are different, and this includes their timelines to reaction to situations of 'extreme gravity'. The new defence allows for a 'cumulative impact' of earlier events to result in a delayed reaction and the defence still be available.

So, whilst a delay is not fatal to a plea of loss of control, it is to be balanced against the fact that the longer the delay, the more scope there is for pre-meditation and acting out of considered revenge, which is fatal to the defence (see below). This was well summarised in the case of **R v Clinton (2012)** where the judge said, 'In reality, the greater the level of deliberation, the less likely it will be that the killing followed a true loss of self-control'.

> **Example: Historical Triggers**
>
> Edith had been subjected to emotional and physical abuse from Jonny, her foster carer as a child. She had not seen Jonny for a number of years. One day, as an adult she was in a park when Jonny approached her from behind causing her shock and panic, he whispered a threat in her ear which referenced the previous abuse he had subjected her to. Edith panicked and was unable to think clearly. She picked up a nearby rock and hit Jonny over the head killing him.
>
> Many of the relevant triggers had occurred many years before, this would not necessarily be fatal to a claim of loss of control under s54(2).

s54 (4) loss of control is unavailable if ... in doing or being party to the killing, D acted in a considered desire for revenge.

This provision clearly establishes when the defence will not available, if the defendant has killed in pursuit of revenge in accordance with a 'considered plan'. This phrase is further not defined within the statute, indicating that this is also a matter that sits for determination with the jury at trial.

The provision suggests that even if a defendant did 'lose control' at the time of killing the defendant, in reaction to what would amount to qualifying triggers, if the defendant has undertaken those acts against the victim purposeful of revenge after time for reflection and consideration, the defence will not be available.

In the case of **R v Jewell (2014)** the trial judge clearly reiterated that revenge within the context of loss of control is a matter for the jury, however it is presumed that considered desire for revenge means a killing 'motivated by a desire to redress or punish some perceived grievance.'

Example: Lawrence's Revenge

Lawrence's friend was killed in a hit and run incident by a drink driver. There were rumours circulating that the drink driver was Norman, a former colleague of Lawrence and his friend. The police were making little progress with the case and Lawrence decided to confront Norman in an attempt to make him confess. He took with him a number of weapons which he was prepared to use to get Norman to admit the truth. Lawrence had no intent on killing Norman, but rather was willing to use force to extract a confession which he would record to send to the Police. When he challenged Norman, Norman laughed at having killed Lawrence's friend and Lawrence lost control and killed him.

Even though Lawrence may have genuinely lost control at the time of killing, the fact he was there to execute a considered desire for revenge means he will be unable to claim the defence under s54(4).

2 Qualifying trigger: Having firstly proved that there was a loss of control at the time of doing the acts that led to the death of the victim, a defendant seeking to rely upon the partial defence of 'loss of control' must prove the loss of control was in reaction to a 'qualifying trigger'.

The word qualifying recognises that a defendant does not have a defence simply because they lost control in reaction to a trigger, the law only recognises certain triggers as 'qualifying', qualifying meaning that there are only a limited set of triggers which the law recognises as justifying the availability of a partial defence to murder.

The law of 'qualifying triggers' is outlined within s55 of the statute.

Statutory reference: S55 Coroners and Justice Act 2009

Meaning of "qualifying trigger"

3. D's loss of self-control was attributable to D's fear of serious violence from V against D or another identified person.

Or;

4. D's loss of self-control was attributable to a thing or things done or said or both which—
   a. constituted circumstances of an extremely grave character, and
   b. caused D to have a justifiable sense of being seriously wronged.

6. In determining whether a loss of self-control had a qualifying trigger—
   a. D's fear of serious violence is to be disregarded if it was caused by a thing which D incited to be done or said for the purpose of providing an excuse to use violence.
   b. a sense of being seriously wronged by a thing done or said is not justifiable if D incited the thing to be done or said for the purpose of providing an excuse to use violence.
   c. the fact that a thing done or said constituted sexual infidelity is to be disregarded.

s55 accordingly creates two qualifying triggers, or a combination of the two will be accepted. The two triggers are commonly recognised as the **fear trigger** and the **anger trigger**.

Exam Gold
For the exam you do not need to rote learn whole sections of statute such as s55, if you are however wanting to achieve the highest marks it is good practice to learn the relevant section numbers that you need and key phrases within the sections. Reciting the key aspects of provisions with accuracy will demonstrate a higher quality answer. Supporting these with further explanation of the nature of the provisions will demonstrate a higher level of understanding.

Fear trigger: s55(3) the defendant feared serious violence from the victim against himself or another identified person.

The first trigger which allows for the defence to be available (where the other two elements are also proven) is where the defendant has lost control in reaction to a fear of serious violence against themselves, or another person.

The act places no limits upon who the other identified person is, for example it does not need to be proved to be family or close friends, but the word 'identified' suggests that a particular person must be specified.

Interestingly, the statute does not state the violence feared has to come from the victim, but this is the predominant course of action.

It is commonly accepted that the test for establishing this qualifying trigger is subjective, this means that the trigger is available where the defendant genuinely believed they or another identified person were in danger of serious violence. It does not have to objectively be proved that a threat of this magnitude did in fact exist.

It is at this point that there is some overlap with the defence of self-defence, as both self-defence and the fear trigger are premised upon the basis of acting in defence of violence from another. Both self-defence and loss of control can be claimed for an offence of murder. Self-defence as a complete R reasonable and proportionate force to threat, loss of control requires proof of a subjective threat of serious violence in response to which there was a killing, a subtle but important distinction.

Anger trigger: s55(4) a thing or things said or done (or both) which:

a **constituted circumstances of an extremely grave character, and;**

b **caused D to have a justifiable sense of being seriously wronged.**

This qualifying trigger initially appears wide in scope, the term 'things said or done' is broad and non-descriptive, however both subsections (a) and (b) must be proved which significantly restrict the availability of what can amount to a trigger under this section. They are further restrictive in the fact that these tests for these two elements are objective.

This trigger is assessed objectively, meaning when considering this trigger, a jury should consider whether the reasonable man regard the circumstances as extremely grave, and would he have felt a justifiable sense of being wronged in the defendant's position?

The adjectives of extremely, justifiable and seriously here worked to emphasise the high objective standard of this test.

Key Case
R v Hatter (2013)

Facts: The defendant and victim were in a relationship, the victim had multiple children from a previous relationship and agreed to a reverse sterilisation to have a child with the defendant. The victim began a sexual relationship with another man. During the night the defendant entered the victim's house with a knife, within the course of an argument the victim was stabbed. The defendant sought to claim that the stabbing and subsequent death was an accident and that he had only taken the knife to pull up the carpets. When prosecuted for murder the judge declined to leave the issue of loss of control to the jury.

Outcome: Appeal dismissed. Guilty of murder

Legal principle: Generally, the breakdown of the relationship will not meet the threshold requirements of the anger trigger to be considered justifiable, although it was recognised that other circumstances can also be considered which may vary this fact.

Key Case
R v Bowyer (2013)

Facts: The defendant and victim were both in a relationship with Katie, a part-time prostitute. The defendant broke into the victim's house in order to conduct a burglary and when the victim returned home, the defendant undertook an attack of a violent nature causing multiple head injuries and blunt force traumas. He tied the victim up and left. The victim subsequently died of his injuries. The defendant claimed that one of the reasons for the attack was that the victim reacted violently to his presence and made a number of upsetting comments about Katie being a prostitute and his 'number one earner', the defendant denied existing knowledge of her prostitution.

Outcome: Guilty of murder

Legal principle: The violent reaction of the victim and insulting references to Katie did not meet the required standards of the anger trigger. These were a reasonable reaction to the presence of a burglar in the home and objectively could not provide the defendant with a basis for claiming they justifiably felt seriously wronged.

Restrictions

In addition to identifying the events, actions or beliefs that can amount to a qualifying trigger, the Act also identifies circumstances where the defence will not be available.

Sections 55(6)(a-b) states that a defendant will not have the defence of loss of control available if he incited (caused / provoked) the victim to do the thing that caused the defendant to have a fear of serious violence, or the thing said or done, if the defendant incited the victim to do that thing for the very purpose that they would then amount to a qualifying trigger and provide the defendant with a defence if they did kill the victim.

Essentially, if the defendant caused or provoked behaviour of the victim to establish qualifying triggers in order to have a justifiable reason to lose control then the defence will not be available, even if in other circumstances the actions would be regarded as a qualifying trigger.

Key Case
R v Dawes (2013)

Facts: The defendant had returned home to find his estranged wife asleep on the sofa with a man that he did not know. The defendant began punching the victim and hitting him with a vodka bottle. The victim took hold of the vodka bottle and tried to attack the defendant, who then went to get a knife and stabbed the victim. The judge did not leave the defence of loss of control to the jury upon the grounds that the defendant had incited the violence, and this prevented the defence being available under the new statute as it meant that there was no available qualifying trigger.

Outcome: Appeal dismissed. Defence not available

Legal principle: Just because a defendant starts a conflict, or is aggressive does not automatically mean the qualifying triggers are not available, ... 'the mere fact that in some general way the defendant was behaving badly and looking for and provoking trouble does not of itself lead to the disapplication of the qualifying triggers.' Though the court did speculate that 'One may wonder (and the judge would have to consider) how often a defendant who is out to incite violence could be said to "fear" serious violence; often he may be welcoming it. Similarly, one may wonder how such a defendant may have a justifiable sense of being seriously wronged if he successfully incites someone else to use violence towards him'.

s55(6)(c) - 'the fact that a thing done or said constituted sexual infidelity is to be disregarded'.

This provision, which was a new principle introduced by the Coroners and Justice Act 2009 excludes sexual infidelity as a qualifying trigger. The Act provided little guidance beyond this, there was no indication about what degree of sexual infidelity had to be proved, or how it had to of been continuing. Even the debates within Parliament during enactment of the provisions gave little indication of what the intended scope of the provision was. It was not therefore until a case upon this point arrived at an appeal court that further common law guidance could be established.

Key Case
R v Clinton (2012)

Facts: The defendant and victim had been married for 16 years and had two children. The victim left the family home alone as part of a trial separation. She had admitted to the defendant that she had been having an affair and had sex with numerous other men. One day she made arrangements to return to the family home to collect some items. Prior to her returning the home the defendant drank and took drugs and found sexually explicit messages and images on her Facebook page, when confronted, she taunted him with graphic details about the sexual encounters. During a subsequent argument she said that she did not want to have the children after their separation and that he did not have the guts to commit suicide, as he had been researching. The defendant killed the victim and then took pictures of her posed semi-naked body and sent them to her lover. At trial the defence of loss of control was not left to the jury due to a misdirection as to the sexual infidelity exclusion, the defendant appealed.

Outcome: Appeal allowed – re-trial ordered*

Legal principle(s):

1. However grave or provocative, sexual infidelity on its own, cannot be recognised as a qualifying trigger in accordance with the statute.
2. Things said or done associated with sexual infidelity are not excluded, for example admissions of sexual infidelity can amount to 'things said' e.g., if a woman came home to find her husband having sex with her sister and then taunted the woman, the words could be a qualifying trigger and the sexual infidelity cannot be ignored.
3. Where there are other qualifying triggers present, alongside sexual infidelity, the context of the sexual infidelity can be considered to determine if the thing said or done meetings the conditions of the qualifying trigger. Whilst the context can be considered, the sexual infidelity still cannot be considered as a trigger.
4. Evidence of sexual infidelity can still be disclosed at trial as it is relevant to the third element of the defence and may be relevant if diminished responsibility is being considered as an alternative defence.

* Prior to the re-trial Clinton entered a guilty plea in relation to the murder charge and was sentenced accordingly. *

3 A person of the D's sex and age, with a normal level of tolerance and self-restraint, in the circumstances of D, would have reacted in the same or similar way:

This third element of the defence introduces a further objective assessment into the availability of loss of control, as clarified in **R v Clinton, Parker & Evans (2012)**, '…even faced with situations which may amount to a qualifying trigger, the defendant is nevertheless expected to exercise a degree of self-control'. This again is a question of fact to be decided by the jury.

This provision considers whether a person of the defendant's sex and age, in those circumstances, but with an ordinary temperament would have had a similar reaction, this is understood to mean the reaction of the reasonable man would be similar, not that the reasonable man would have lost control.

Key Case
R v Christian (2018)

Facts: The defendant lived in a shared house with the first victim, they got into a verbal dispute, later that evening continued with the first and second victim, and the second victim's two sons. The defendant stabbed all four of them during the conflict, the first and second victim died from multiple significant wounds and the two sons sustained severe injuries. The defendant claimed he was defending himself from attack from the four others and could not recall use of the knife or stabbing the others. The judge refused to allow the defence of loss of control to be left to the jury.

Outcome: Guilty of murder. Defence failed

Legal principle: Whilst a reasonable person in the defendant's circumstances may have reacted by using significant force in self-defence, the attack conducted by the defendant and his behaviour was so extreme that no jury could conclude that a person of the defendant's sex and age would have reacted in the same or similar way.

Whilst it is a largely objective test, there are subjective elements contained within it, firstly the defendant's sex and age are relevant, this recognises that a person's sex and age may affect the reaction that they have.

The 'circumstances of the D' further introduces a subjective element, this means that the situation of the defendant, the qualifying triggers, and any sexual infidelity can be considered as a circumstance of the defendant, however the statute does restrict the relevance of some circumstances.

s54(3) In subsection (1)(c) the reference to "the circumstances of D" is a reference to all of D's circumstances other than those whose only relevance to D's conduct is that they bear on D's general capacity for tolerance or self-restraint.

Factors that the courts have previously concluded to be excluded under this provision are a mental disorder of the defendant if it affects their ability to exercise self-control, any voluntary intoxication of the defendant, and any general character traits such as if the defendant was a particularly volatile or irrational individual.

> **Example: Adrian's Extreme Reaction**
>
> Adrian was an elderly gentleman who suffered from depression which caused aggressive episodes. One day he became involved in an altercation in a car park with a teenager. The teenager admitted that he was part of the gang that had been tormenting Adrian for a number of years with hoax calls, criminal damage and spreading malicious rumours. Adrian lost control and deliberately ran the teenager over in the car park. Having ran him over he reversed his car and kept on running his car over him despite the fact he was on the floor defenceless.
>
> The reaction of Adrian here was so extreme, a jury may conclude that the third element of the test is not proved as no person of the D's sex and age would have reacted in such a way, further as Adrian's depression appears only to affect his ability to exercise self-control, it would likely not be accepted as a 'circumstance of the defendant'.

Diminished responsibility

The defence of diminished responsibility, like the defence of provocation, was introduced in the **Homicide Act 1957** and is contained in **s2(1)**. When the area of voluntary manslaughter was subject reform by the **Coroners and Justice Act 2009**, the defence was not abolished and replaced, but rather updated, the updates were outlined within **s52 Coroners and Justice Act 2009**.

The full citation for reference is therefore **s2(1) Homicide Act 1957** as amended by the **Coroners and Justice Act 2009**. Diminished responsibility like the defence of loss of control is a special and partial defence. There are four elements of the defence, all of which must be proved in order for the defence to be available.

> **The test for diminished responsibility**
>
> 1 The defendant was suffering from an **abnormality of mental functioning** which;
> 2 Arose from a **recognised medical condition**;
> 3 That **substantially impaired** the defendant's ability to; (a) understand the nature of D's conduct; (b) form a rational judgment or; (c) exercise self-control and;
> 4 **Provides an explanation** for the defendant's acts / omissions in doing or being a party to the killing.

1 Abnormality of mental functioning

The first element of the defence requires the jury to determine as a question of fact, rather than medicine, whether the defendant's state of mind at the time of killing was 'abnormal'.

The phrase under the **Homicide Act 1957** was 'abnormality of mind' and was updated to 'mental functioning' by the **Coroners and Justice Act 2009**, neither statute sought to define this term, we therefore must rely upon the common law definition as provided by the courts.

Key Case
R v Byrne (1960)

Facts: In a hostel, the defendant strangled a young woman and then mutilated her body, The defendant admitted the killing but sought to rely upon the defence of diminished responsibility. Medical evidence supported the finding that the defendant was a sexual psychopath, and this caused an abnormality of mind at the time of the killing, he was unable to control his sexual desires.

Outcome: Guilty of voluntary manslaughter. Defence successful

Legal principle: An abnormality of mental functioning '…. means a state of mind so different from that of ordinary human beings that the reasonable man would term it abnormal'. This is a question of fact for the jury to determine in line with medical and all other evidence presented by the case.

It has been confirmed by the courts on a number of occasions that this definition still applies to the phrase 'abnormality of mental functioning', despite the slight change in wording as Parliament chose not to provide a definition in the **Coroners and Justice Act 2009.**

Exam Gold In an application question, you will need to make a judgment about whether the D has an abnormality of mental functioning based upon the facts you are presented. You must draw a conclusion upon whether the defendant's state of mind is abnormal, it is important that you distinguish this from their act's being abnormal, which is not the focus of abnormality of mental functioning. It is important to note that Byrne (1960) uses the phrase 'so different from an ordinary man', a slightly abnormal state of mind may not be sufficient to meet this criterion.

Example: Niamh's Schizophrenia

Niamh suffered from schizophrenia since she was a child. This would cause her to suffer psychotic episodes where she would have vivid hallucinations that her life was under threat by killer aliens. Niamh worked closely with her medical team and was taking medication which controlled her condition. Niamh got into an argument at a festival and killed another person. If it could not be proved that she was suffering from a psychotic episode at the time of the killing she would not have the defence available, whilst she had a recognised medical condition capable of causing an abnormality, if it was not operational at the time of the acts that have caused the victim's death the defence is not available.

2 Recognised medical condition

Once the state of mind requirements of 'abnormality of mental functioning' have been proved, it must be established that the cause of this is a recognised medical condition, rather than a state of intoxication for example. The link between these two is important to establish as a basis for the defence.

The term 'recognised medical condition' is wide and not defined in the statute. At trial the presence of a recognised medical condition, or lack of will be supported by expert witnesses, who can be presented by both the prosecution and defence. Just because there is an accepted recognised medical condition present does not automatically mean the defence is available, the remaining elements may still remain unproven.

The CPS states the recognised medical conditions can be found in the 'World Health Organisation's International Classification of Diseases (ICD-10) and the American Psychiatric Association's Diagnostic and Statistical Manual of Mental Disorders (DSM-IV)' - **https://www.cps.gov.uk/legal-guidance/homicide-murder-and-manslaughter**

This term despite relating to the mind of the defendant is not limited to just psychiatric or psychological conditions but can also include physical health conditions, provided they have caused an 'abnormality of mental functioning'.

Examples have included:
- **R v Byrne (1960):** sexual psychopathy.
- **R v Conroy (2017):** autism spectrum disorder.
- **R v Dietschmann (2003):** adjustment disorder.
- **R v Ahluwalia (1993):** battered spouse syndrome
- **R v Martin (Anthony) (2001):** depression
- **R v Reynolds (1988):** pre-menstrual tension
- **R v Campbell (1997):** epilepsy
- **R v Wood (2008):** alcohol dependency syndrome.

Key Case
R v Dowds (2012)

Facts: The defendant and his partner (the victim), regularly drank large volumes of alcohol. He was not alcohol dependent but described himself as a 'heavy but elective drinker'. Whilst intoxicated they would often get into physical and violent altercations. On one occasion, the defendant inflicted around 60 knife wounds on the victim which caused her death, whilst he was intoxicated. He had no recollection of the incident and sought to rely upon diminished responsibility on the grounds that his temporary state of voluntary intoxication at the time of her killing was a recognised medical condition. Whilst this would not have been accepted prior to the updates by the Coroners and Justice Act 2009, he sought to argue that the change to the law included his intoxicated state to form the basis of the defence. As this was the only ground to base diminished responsibility upon, the trial judge did not put the defence to the jury.

Outcome: Convicted of murder. No defence allowed

Legal principle: The changes to the law by the 2009 Act did not amend the well-established common law rule that voluntary acute intoxication, not linked to alcoholism is not a recognised medical condition for the purposes of diminished responsibility. This principle would equally apply to the voluntary ingestion of drugs.

Exam Gold In an application question it is important that you are able to distinguish between the abnormality of mental functioning and the recognised medical condition. The recognised medical condition is the diagnosable condition the defendant has, the abnormality is the abnormal state of mind the defendant had at the time of killing caused by the condition. Just because there is a medical condition does not automatically mean there is an abnormal state of mind.

Example: Rodger's Severe Depression

Roger had suffered from severe depression for a number of years for which he was prescribed medication. Despite the medication, Roger's depression meant that he would often suffer from aggressive rages and be volatile in an otherwise calm situation. One day during an argument at the pub, Roger punched Jon repeatedly until he was unconscious. Jon eventually died from the injuries. If prosecuted for murder Roger may seek to rely upon diminished responsibility, the abnormality being the aggressive rages, the recognised medical condition being the condition that has caused this.

Exam Gold When seeking to identify a recognised medical condition in an exam question, the examiners are not expecting you to make a formal diagnosis. In some scenario questions the examiner will give you the name of a condition e.g., anxiety, depression, paranoia, schizophrenia, multiple sclerosis, bipolar disorder, epilepsy or a brain tumour. Sometimes the scenario will not state a condition but will indicate no other cause of the abnormal mind e.g., intoxication by drunk or drugs. Where this is the case, you do not need to speculate about what condition may be present, but rather suggest in the absence of any other cause of the abnormality that it is presumed the condition is present.

3 Substantial impairment

Once it has been established that the defendant has a medical condition which has caused an abnormality, it must further be proved that the abnormality substantially impaired the defendant's mind in one of three ways:

a **to understand the nature of his conduct**
b **to form a rational judgement; or**
c **to exercise self-control**

It is important to note that the abnormality must only substantially impair the defendant in one of these three ways not all of them. The three criteria are outlined within the statute.

The use of the word substantial also means that it does not have to be proved that one of the three mental abilities has been totally impaired, rather substantially.

Key Case
R v Golds (2014)

Facts: The defendant admitted causing the death of his partner via the infliction of of 22 wounds and blunt force injuries. He sought to rely upon the defence of diminished responsibility at trial. When the Police arrived at the scene the defendant was described as appearing deranged and 'snarling like an animal'. The defendant suffered from ongoing mental disorders and psychiatric evidence supported the finding of an abnormality caused by a recognised medical condition. In the summing up at trial the judge declined to provide the jury with guidance upon the term 'substantial' and the defendant appealed contending that a direction upon the meaning of the word should have been given.

Outcome: Convicted of murder

Legal principle: the phrase substantial in this context does not mean a more than trivial impairment but means 'important or weighty', also phrased as 'an impairment of consequence or weight'.

Key Case
R v Conroy (2017)

Facts: The defendant had a difficult upbringing and was taken into care. he had a diagnosis of ASD (Autistic Spectrum Disorder) and ADHD (Attention Deficit Hyperactive Disorder) and displayed violent sexualised behaviours. At the time of the offence the defendant lived in a specialist home for people with ASD, as did the victim. During one evening the defendant admitted going into her room, strangling her and then trying to drag her to his room in order to have sex with her. He dropped her on the way to his room which alerted staff who found her unconscious. She later died as a result of his attack. Psychiatrists presented varying rationales for the events and the judge directed that this was for the jury to determine. Whilst all experts agreed there was an abnormality caused by the ASD, there was dispute as to whether this led to a substantial impairment.

Outcome: Guilty of murder

Legal principle: The defendant undertook a planned and premeditated attack which was designed to avoid detection by staff at the home. Whilst the defendant was motivated by his existing desires caused by his ASD, he was aware that his attacks were wrong yet undertook them anyway, this was not a substantial impairment of an ability to form a rational judgment, he was thinking of a rational way to execute his plan. The phrase 'form a rational judgment' refers to the defendant's ability to come to a rational judgment but may also include an assessment by a jury of their ability to think rationally to make a judgment, to distinguish the two is to over-refine the law.

4 Provides an explanation for the conduct

The fourth element of the defence requires proof that the abnormality caused by the recognised medical condition, which has caused the substantial impairment has either caused or is a significant factor in causing the defendant to kill. It is important to recognise that the four elements of this defence are inherently interconnected and do not stand alone as independent tests.

This fourth element was a new requirement introduced by the **Coroners and Justice Act 2009** and involves the jury making an assessment of the reasons why the defendant killed, the defence will only be available if they feel that at the time the defendant killed, the abnormality was one of the significant reasons. Therefore, it need not be proved that the abnormality of mental functioning is the only cause (reason) the defendant took part in the killing, there may be other reasons the defendant killed which do not prevent the defence from being available, however the abnormality must be a significant factor.

Section 1B Homicide Act 1957: '… an abnormality of mental functioning provides an explanation for D's conduct if it causes or is a **significant contributory factor** in causing, D to carry out that conduct'.

Example: Imran's Revenge

Imran was a member of a notorious gang who were well known for violence and drugs. Imran had been convicted of multiple violent offences. One day he was looking for Delal, a rival gang member, as Delal had been selling drugs in an area that was well known to be ran by Imran's gang. Imran discovered that Delal had also been dating his sister secretly, which significantly aggravated him. Imran found Delal in a bar and they got into an intense argument, a fight began, and Imran stamped on Delal's head multiple times, including whilst he was unconscious on the floor causing his death. Imran's defence team produced medical evidence at trial that Imran had a medical condition that made him aggressive and volatile.

When assessing whether the abnormality is a significant contributory factor the courts would consider whether it was a significant cause within the context of the other reasons Imran killed, i.e. he had a history of violent behaviour, he was undertaking a seemingly planned attack, motivated by Delal's drug dealing in his area and having found out that he dated his sister.

A jury may justifiably conclude in these circumstances that the abnormality was not a significant cause, rather he was clearly motivated by revenge.

Exam Gold In an application question, this is a difficult element to apply. You should discuss all of the factors presented by the scenario that are suggested as reasons why the defendant killed. You should then have a reasoned discussion upon which appear to be the most significant reasons, remembering the defence will only succeed where the abnormality is one of these significant factors. Do remember that this will be a hypothetical discussion, you only have a few lines of information, and this is a fictional scenario, providing a reasoned conclusion upon the limited facts will get you the marks you require.

Effect of intoxication upon the availability of diminished responsibility as a defence

It has been long established by law that being temporarily voluntarily intoxicated, whether by drink or drugs is not a recognised medical condition and is not capable of founding the defence of diminished responsibility. The issue is much more complicated where the defendant is both intoxicated and suffering from an abnormality at the time of killing, even further where the recognised medical condition is alcoholism.

The defendant is intoxicated and suffering from an unrelated abnormality of mental functioning at the time of carrying out the killing:

Key Case
R v Dietschmann (2003)

Facts: The defendant killed the victim in a violent attack, whilst he was intoxicated and suffering from an abnormality caused by a medical condition, as was supported by medical evidence at the trial. His medical condition was an adjustment disorder following the death of his aunt whom he had a close and intimate relationship with. The incident arose because the defendant accused the victim of breaking his watch, the last present from his aunt. As the attack was prior to 2010, he sought to rely upon diminished responsibility in its original form, prior to the 2010 updates. At the trial the judge directed the jury that the defence would only be available where it could be proved that the defendant would have killed without the drink due to his abnormality. The defendant appealed to the House of Lords upon the basis that this was a misdirection.

Outcome: Appeal allowed, and a re-trial was ordered

Legal principle: In cases where the defendant is both intoxicated and acting under diminished responsibility at the time of killing, the question for the jury to determine is 'despite the drink, his mental abnormality substantially impaired his mental responsibility for his fatal acts, or has he failed to satisfy you of that?' This does not require the defendant to prove that he would have killed without the drink, there may be some cases where it is concluded that a defendant has killed because of the combination of the intoxicant and the abnormality, provided it can still be proved that the abnormality was a significant factor in killing, this does not prevent the defence from being available.

This test means that effectively a jury has to ignore the effects of the voluntary intoxication and they cannot be considered when trying to determine if the defendant had an abnormality of mental functioning.

It has been accepted by the courts that this is the correct approach to follow even after the updates to the defence made by the **Coroners and Justice Act 200**9 as was demonstrated in the case of **R v Joyce and Kay (2017)**.

> **Exam Gold** If an application question presents you with facts that suggest a defendant is intoxicated at the time of killing (but not dependent on alcohol) and suffering from an abnormality of mental functioning, you must apply the principles in R v Dietschmann (2003). Begin by recognising the intoxication, and outline the test from the case, then continue to consider whether the elements of diminished responsibility are present 'despite the drink'. You will then conclude discussion of diminished responsibility and the intoxication under element four of the defence by discussing which, and remember it can be both, was a significant factor in causing the defendant to kill.

The defendant is intoxicated at the time of killing and suffers from the recognised medical conditions 'alcohol dependency syndrome':

This particular circumstance, where the defendant is intoxicated at the time of killing but their intoxication is due to alcoholism (a recognised medical condition), presents the most complex combination of intoxication and diminished responsibility. The primary question for concern here is whether the effects of the intoxication should be considered within the abnormality.

The law suggests there are two ways in this circumstances that a jury can consider the effects of the alcohol consumed within the context of the abnormality, firstly if the alcoholism has caused brain damage or a condition such as psychosis, or secondly, if the drinking has become involuntary. There has been some dispute within the common law as to what constitutes involuntary drinking within this context.

The issue was concisely referenced in the case of **R v Diestchmann (2003)** where it was stated that **'R v Tandy (1989)** established that drink is only capable of giving rise to a defence under section 2 if it either causes damage to the brain or produces an irresistible craving so that consumption is involuntary'.

50 **OCR A-Level Law Criminal Law Study Book 1**

Key Case
R v Wood (2008)

Facts: The defendant killed the victim in a frenzied attack hitting him 37 times with a meat cleaver after discovering the victim attempting to perform an act of oral sex upon him. At the time of the attack the defendant was heavily intoxicated and suffering from alcohol dependency syndrome (ADS), the former being supported by medical evidence at the trial. The defendant's life had become consumed by alcohol, and he would spend every waking moment thinking about and trying to acquire drink. The judge directed the jury to ignore the effects of any voluntary intoxication and only consider the effects of the alcohol within the abnormality if it is regarded as involuntary. He further went on to state that drinking was only involuntary where a person could not act otherwise, simply giving in to a craving was not involuntary consumption. The defendant appealed upon the basis that this was a misdirection.

Outcome: Appeal allowed – conviction reduced to voluntary manslaughter.

Legal principle: Where brain damage has occurred as a consequence of ADS a jury may conclude that this presents the abnormality of mental functioning. Even where there is no brain damage, a defendant in these circumstances may still have the defence available, a jury can consider the effects of the drinking within the abnormality, but within this context could only consider the effects of drinking as a result of the alcoholism, not drink that has been voluntarily consumed. It does not have to be proved that every drink of the day was involuntary for this to be applicable as was suggested at trial.

Exam Gold In an application question you should only dedicate your limited time to issues that are presented for discussion. If you are discussing diminished responsibility and the issue is not complicated by the presence of any intoxication, there is no value in mentioning any of the principles. You do not get marks in application questions for discussing issues that are not presented for application.

Key Terms – Fatal Offences Against the Person - Voluntary Manslaughter

Homicide	The killing of one human being by another.
Voluntary manslaughter	A verdict that can be delivered where a defendant successfully pleads a partial defence to murder, namely loss of control or diminished responsibility.
Partial defence	A defence that if successfully used does not result in an acquittal but a reduced conviction.
Special defence	A defence that is only available to one offence.
Loss of control	A partial defence to murder contained within and introduced by the Coroners and Justice Act 2009.
Considered desire for revenge	Undertaking actions for the purpose of revenge and retribution may prevent the defence of loss of control being available where the defendant kills the victim, even if at the time the defendant did lose control.
Qualifying trigger	An event or belief that must be proved to have caused the defendant's loss of control in order for the defence to be available.
Fear trigger	A fear by the defendant of serious violence against themselves or another identified person, a subjective test.
Anger trigger	A thing or things said or done which are objectively of an extremely grave character and have caused the defendant to have a justifiable sense of feeling seriously wronged.
Sexual infidelity	Where a person is unfaithful to a partner in a sexual manner, this is excluded as a qualifying trigger for the purposes of loss of control within the statute.
Diminished responsibility	A partial defence to murder based upon recognition of a recognised medical condition that if successful, results in a verdict of voluntary manslaughter that does not carry a mandatory life sentence.
Abnormality of mental functioning	The first element of diminished responsibility, a state of mind that is so different from an ordinary human beings that the reasonable man would term it abnormal.

Continued on next page

Key Terms – Fatal Offences Against the Person - Voluntary Manslaughter

Recognised medical condition	In order to claim diminished responsibility, the defence at trial must present medical evidence to establish that a defendant has a medical condition that has caused the abnormality of mental functioning at the time the defendant killed the victim.
Substantial impairment	The abnormality of mental functioning must be proved to have substantially impaired the defendant's mental ability in one of three ways at the time of killing the victim. Substantial means 'important or weighty'.
Provides an explanation	For the defence of diminished responsibility, it must be proved that the defendant's abnormality of mental functioning either caused or was a significant contributory factor in causing the defendant to kill.

One Sentence Case Summary – Fatal Offences Against the Person - Voluntary Manslaughter – Loss of Control

Name	Topic Link	Legal significance
R v Jewell (2014)	Loss of control	It is the role of the judge to determine if there is sufficient evidence to put loss of control to the jury, whilst the term 'loss of control' is not defined in the statute, the academic definition of '… a loss of the ability to act in accordance with considered judgment or a loss of normal powers of reasoning' is acceptable.
		Whilst the issues of considered desire for revenge is one to be determined by the jury, it is assumed to mean acts 'motivated by a desire to redress or punish some perceived grievance.'
R v Dawes, Hatter and Bowyer (2013)	Loss of control – reaction need not be sudden	Any delay between the qualifying trigger(s) and the loss of control does not render the defence void, the defence is still available where a defendant later reacts to the 'cumulative impact' of earlier events.
R v Clinton (2012)	Loss of control – reaction need not be sudden	The increase in a delay between the qualifying triggers increases the likelihood of premeditation and decreases the likelihood of a loss of control truly being present.
R v Hatter (2013)	Loss of control – anger trigger	Generally, the breakdown of the relationship will not meet the threshold requirements of the anger trigger, although it was recognised that other circumstances can also be considered which may vary this fact.
R v Bowyer (2013)	Loss of control – anger trigger	A defendant was unable to prove a justifiable sense of being seriously wronged where he broke into the victim's home and the victim responded in a violent and insulting manner. These reasonable reactions of the victim to the presence of a burglar (the defendant) in their home objectively could not provide the defendant with a basis for claiming they justifiably felt seriously wronged.
R v Dawes (2013)	Loss of control – qualifying triggers	Just because the defendant is generally behaving badly and / or provoking trouble does not automatically mean the qualifying triggers are disqualified under ss55(6) (a-b).
R v Clinton (2012)	Loss of control – sexual infidelity	Sexual infidelity alone cannot be recognised as a qualifying trigger, things said or done associated with sexual infidelity and the context of the infidelity are not disregarded, further sexual infidelity is still relevant to the third element of the defence.
R v Christian (2018)	Loss of control – third part of the test	A defendant will not have the defence of loss of control available where it is concluded that a person of the defendant's sex and age would not have reacted in the extreme way the defendant did.

One Sentence Case Summary – Fatal Offences Against the Person - Voluntary Manslaughter – Diminished Responsibility		
Name	**Topic Link**	**Legal significance**
R v Byrne (1960)	Diminished responsibility – abnormality of mental functioning	An abnormality of mind is a 'state of mind so different from that of an ordinary human being that the reasonable man would term it abnormal', this is a matter for the jury to decide.
R v Dowds (2012)	Diminished responsibility – recognised medical condition	Voluntary acute intoxication, unlinked to dependency, whether caused by drink or drugs, does not form the basis of a recognised medical condition for the purpose of diminished responsibility, this was the case before and after the updates to the law by the 2009 Act.
R v Golds (2014)	Diminished responsibility – substantial impairment	The phrase substantial means, important, weighty or an impairment of consequence.
R v Conroy (2017)	Diminished responsibility – ability to form a rational judgment	The phrase 'form a rational judgment' refers to the defendant's ability to come to a rational judgment but may also include an assessment by a jury of their ability to think rationally to make a judgment, to distinguish the two is to over-refine the law.
R v Dietschmann (2003)	Diminished responsibility – abnormality and intoxication	Where a defendant is intoxicated and suffering from an abnormality at the time of killing, a jury should consider whether the abnormality substantially impaired the defendants' mental abilities, despite the drink, even where it is concluded that a defendant may not have killed without the drink, it may still be concluded the defence is available.
R v Joyce Kay (2017)	Diminished responsibility – abnormality and intoxication	It was confirmed that the principles laid down in R v Dietschmann (2003) regarding alcohol consumption and a separate abnormality continue to apply after the changes to the law made by the Coroners and Justice Act 2009.
R v Tandy (1989)	Diminished responsibility – alcohol dependency syndrome	The consumption of alcohol is only capable of founding a defence of diminished responsibility if it either causes brain damage or produces an 'irresistible craving so that consumption is involuntary'.
R v Wood (2008)	Diminished responsibility – alcohol dependency syndrome	The fundamental principles of R v Tandy (1989) remain, there are two ways that alcoholism can form the basis of an abnormality, where it has caused brain damage of the consumption of alcohol is involuntary, for the later it does not have to be proved that all of the defendant's drinking was involuntary.

FATAL OFFENCES AGAINST THE PERSON - INVOLUNTARY MANSLAUGHTER

Exam Reference:	H418/01 – The Legal System and Criminal Law (Paper 1)
	Involuntary manslaughter is a substantive topic that appears in paper 1 of the OCR Law A-Level exam series. 60 marks out of 80 are allocated to substantive law topics in this paper. You will be required to accurately identify and explain the principles of involuntary manslaughter (AO1) which includes unlawful act manslaughter and gross negligence manslaughter and apply them to scenario-based questions (AO2).'
Topic Content:	• Unlawful act manslaughter • Gross negligence manslaughter

Topic overview

The involuntary manslaughter offences sit within the law of unlawful homicide, the killing of one person by another unlawfully. Similar to the law of murder, the two offences require proof that the defendant caused the death of the victim, both factually and legally? (discussed in chapter one.) The phrase manslaughter denotes that the defendant caused the death without the required intention for murder (although voluntary manslaughter is an exception to this rule as you can be convicted of voluntary manslaughter with an intent to kill). The term involuntary here is particularly misleading, the offences are not committed in an uncontrolled way. There is a common misconception that manslaughter is accidental death, if a death is truly accidental and there is no fault with regard the person who has contributed toward the death, there may be no criminal liability, though this is unlikely to be present in a Law exam.

Both offences are contained entirely within the common law and have never been subject to statutory definition. They are both indictable and thus can only be tried at the Crown Court, and whilst they hold a maximum sentence of life imprisonment, this is not mandatory, and the court maintains a significant amount of discretion when sentencing.

There are two main forms of involuntary manslaughter, namely manslaughter by an unlawful act and manslaughter by gross negligence. There is a third form, subjective recklessness manslaughter, its existence is actually now in dispute, but this is not covered by the OCR specification.

Unlawful Act Manslaughter

Unlawful act manslaughter also referred to as '**constructive manslaughter**' is an offence that requires proof that the defendant committed an unlawful and dangerous act (separate criminal offence) and that caused the death of the victim. The offence is also known as constructive manslaughter, this is because liability for the manslaughter offence is constructed (justified, created from) from an initial offence which they must have committed, both actus reus and mens rea in order to be found guilty.

This makes the offence of unlawful act manslaughter extremely wide, and its scope covers a wide range of circumstances, there are few limits on what the initial unlawful act can be, and liability can be constructed from a very minor offence. There are four elements to the offence, three elements of actus reus and one of mens rea, all of which must be proven in order to establish liability.

Elements of the offence:

Actus reus	Mens rea
1 The defendant commits an **unlawful act** 2 The unlawful act is **dangerous**. 3 The unlawful act **caused the death of the victim.**	4 The defendant has the **mens rea for the initial unlawful act.**

1 Unlawful act

The first element of unlawful act manslaughter requires proof that the defendant committed a separate criminal offence, not just the causing of the victim's death, but they have committed some other criminal act contrary to law.

> **Exam Gold** In the exam this will usually be an alternative offence that is covered within the specification, for example a non-fatal offence, a theft or a robbery. Although the offence itself is not restricted to these offences. If you know the initial unlawful act, give a basic explanation and application of the AR, if you are not familiar with the offence e.g., if it was criminal damage, simply identify the offence and discuss where you think the actus reus is proved.

The common law has introduced some restrictions on what may suffice as an initial unlawful act, although no specific offences are excluded. However logically, an offence which has mens rea which will satisfy murder cannot be the initial unlawful act, as if an intent to kill or cause GBH is proved alongside the defendant factually and legally causing the death of the victim, the relevant offence for discussion is murder not manslaughter. In accordance with this an offence of GBH or wounding under **s18 OAPA 1861** cannot be the initial unlawful act, as the mens rea requires intention that would satisfy a murder conviction.

A further restriction upon the initial unlawful act is that is cannot be committed by omission, this is clearly emphasised by the word act within the title. If a defendant does cause a death that does not amount to murder by omission, they may be guilty of the alternative involuntary manslaughter offence of gross negligence manslaughter.

A conviction of unlawful act manslaughter cannot be proved if there is no initial unlawful act. Further, a charge of unlawful act manslaughter may be disproved if the defendant is able to rely upon a defence with regard the initial unlawful act.

Key Case
R v Lamb (1967)

Facts: The defendant, a 25-year-old male, whilst joking around with his best friend (the victim), aimed and fired a revolver at his best friend causing his death. There was no intention to kill or cause harm, neither friend believed there was a bullet in the next firing chamber. The incident was defended as a genuine accident.

Outcome: Not guilty

Legal principle: For manslaughter to be proved the initial unlawful act must technically satisfy the actus reus and mens rea of a criminal offence, this was not proved in this case.

Example: One punch killing

Paula became involved in a fight with Sarah, whilst at a festival. Paula and Sarah had previously been friends for years, but Paula had just discovered that Sarah had been having an affair with her boyfriend. Paula found Sarah in her tent and confronted her, an argument ensued and Paula, upset by Sarah's comments punched her once then ran away crying. Sarah's friends presumed that she was too upset to come out of her tent as she would not respond to their texts, so they left her until the following morning, when Sarah was found dead having suffered a bleed on the brain following the punch.

In circumstances like these Paula would not be prosecuted for murder as a single punch does not demonstrate even indirect intention to cause GBH. Paula would most likely be prosecuted for unlawful act manslaughter upon the basis of an initial offence of battery (the punch) for which she had actus reus and mens rea, which then went on to cause the death of the victim.

It is also of importance to note that the initial unlawful act must be an offence contrary to the criminal law, not a breach of any other area of law such as negligence in tort or breach in contract law.

> ## Key Case
> ## Andrews v DPP (1937)
> **Facts:** The defendant whilst overtaking a car was on the wrong side of the road and hit a pedestrian. The defendant drove off from the scene, did not alert the emergency services and as a consequence the pedestrian died. The defendant was convicted of manslaughter and appealed upon the basis that there was a technical misdirection at trial.
>
> **Outcome:** Appeal dismissed, and conviction upheld
>
> **Legal principle:** Negligent acts that would usually constitute civil liability cannot satisfy an offence of unlawful act manslaughter. Criminal acts constitute an unlawful act for the purpose of unlawful act manslaughter.

It is also important to note that the initial unlawful act does not have to be an offence against the person, despite the fact that the overarching offence of unlawful act manslaughter is.

> ## Key Case
> ## R v Farnon and Ellis (2015)
> **Facts:** Two defendants aged 14 and 16 were inside a derelict building, they started a fire which they left, the fire caused the death of a homeless man squatting within the building. Their conviction of unlawful act manslaughter was founded upon the initial unlawful act of arson, an offence against property.
>
> **Outcome:** Guilty
>
> **Legal principle:** The initial unlawful act is not limited to offences against the person and can include other offences, such as offences against property.

> **Example: Unlawful Acts**
>
> Example offences that may be proof of an initial unlawful act – assault, battery, ABH, GBH / wounding s20, theft, robbery, burglary, blackmail, criminal damage, criminal damage by arson, affray, disorderly behaviour.

2 Dangerousness

It is not sufficient to simply prove the defendant committed a criminal act that caused death, it must further be proved that the initial unlawful act was also **objectively dangerous**. The law has not established a list of offences which are / are not dangerous, rather, the common law has developed a generic test that can be applied to the circumstances of any offence to identify if it satisfies the criteria of 'dangerousness'. The test of dangerousness can therefore be applied to any offence to determine if this element is proved or not. As discussed with reference to the initial unlawful act, the unlawful act can be any criminal offence, so there is no limit upon what acts can be regarded as dangerous, as confirmed in **R v Willoughby (2005)** the initial unlawful act can be an offence against property and still be dangerous to a person.

Key Case
R v Church (1966)

Facts: The defendant and victim engaged in a sexual encounter in his van, she slapped him after he was unable to satisfy her needs, leading him to carry out a brutal and violent attack on her. Following the attack, she was unconscious, and the defendant was unable to wake her, mistakenly believing she was dead he threw her body in a nearby river, a post-mortem revealed she was in fact alive at this point and died from subsequently drowning as a result of being thrown in the river.

Outcome: Guilty

Legal principle: An unlawful act causing death is not enough to found a conviction in manslaughter, it must be proved that the act was dangerous which means 'the unlawful act must be such as all sober and reasonable people would inevitably recognise must subject the other person to, at least, the risk of some harm resulting therefrom, albeit not serious harm'.

The key test is therefore, **'would the reasonable man foresee the risk of some physical harm to another as a consequence of the unlawful act?'**

Exam Gold When applying the test of dangerousness within the exam you should look to the circumstances of the initial unlawful act and discuss whether or not there is objectively a risk of harm to any person (not just the victim) as a consequence of the act. Consider how the offence was committed, the environment the offence occurred in, what articles / items were involved, all of these factors are relevant the risk of physical harm to the another as a consequence of the defendant's unlawful act.

It is important to note that this test is **objective**, it is only concerned with the foresight of the reasonable man, it is irrelevant for a defendant to claim that their liability should be reduced or affected because they themselves did not foresee a risk of harm, their foresight is irrelevant. The courts have developed generic principles upon what knowledge is attributed to the reasonable person when applying this test.

Key Case
R v Dawson (1985)

Facts: Two defendants carried out an armed burglary of a petrol station, the staff member working in the petrol station died of a heart attack as a consequence of the burglary. Medical evidence later proved that the victim had a pre-existing heart condition which was not known to the defendants. The weapons used by the defendants were replicas and the defendants had no knowledge of the heart condition of the victim.

Outcome: Not guilty

Legal principle: Unknown conditions of the victims cannot be considered when determining dangerousness if they are not known at the time, dangerousness must be determined by the viewpoint of the reasonable man watching the events unfold, with the knowledge of the defendant but no more, in this case the knowledge of the heart condition could not be taken into consideration when determining dangerousness, it was not known by the defendants therefore could not be known by the reasonable man.

Key Case
R v Farnon and Ellis (2015)

Facts: Two defendants aged 14 and 16 were inside a derelict building, they started a fire which they left, the fire caused the death of a homeless man squatting within the building. The 14-year-old had a particularly low IQ and professionals advised that he had the mental capacity of a six-year-old. When directing the jury upon the issue of dangerousness the trial judge stated that 'It is immaterial whether or not the defendant actually knew or actually realised that the act was dangerous. The defendants appealed contending that the test of dangerousness should be adapted to reflect their age and the reduced mental capacity of Farnon.

Outcome: Guilty

Legal principle: The direction of the trial judge was correct; the test is completely objective and should not be subjectively adjusted to the individual circumstances of the offenders.

Key Case
R v JM and another (2012)

Facts: The victim was a doorman, aged 40, with no known existing medical conditions. The two defendants were in the nightclub where the victim was working early one morning. They were asked to leave and escorted out the fire door and were descending the stairs. One of the defendants went back up the stairs and kicked the door. Doormen, including the victim came out and became involved in a physical altercation with the two defendants. When ascending the stairs after the incident the victim collapsed and died from a pre-existing but unknown aneurysm. Medical evidence proved that this was caused by the increased in blood pressure following the incident. The defence contended that harm of this form was not foreseeable to the reasonable man and therefore the test of dangerousness was not satisfied.

Outcome: Guilty

Legal principle: The test of dangerousness does not demand that the reasonable man must foresee that type of physical harm from which the victim ultimately dies, it is enough that they foresee the risk of some physical harm occurring from the unlawful act. In this case is therefore did not matter that the specific harm that caused the death of the victim was not foreseeable, because the risk of some harm from the altercation was foreseeable.

Key Case
R v Larkin (1943)

Facts: The defendant went to find his partner and found her drinking with three others, he left annoyed at the situation and brooded on it, he then returned to the group armed with his razor. The defendant claimed to be annoyed at one of the men she was drinking with and took the razor to scare him with, it was claimed that whilst attempting to scare the man, his partner, intoxicated by drink fell against the razor that was in his hand.

Outcome: Guilty

Legal principle: Where a defendant commits an unlawful act against one person and that act is dangerous to another, they are still guilty of manslaughter where that dangerous act causes the death of another 'quite inadvertently'.

Example: Flora's Threats

Flora and her friends, a group of students were drinking on their local playing fields one summer evening. Angela, a girl from college who they disliked was walking through the field at the time. Flora stood up and shouted at Angela 'you better run mangy Angie or else I am going to give you a black eye' (a technical assault). Flora and her friends then laughed, having no intention of carrying out any attack and watched Angela leave the field. Angela ran all the way home and went to bed feeling unwell, she died in her sleep from extreme dehydration from the run.

A jury would likely conclude that the unlawful act of assault was not dangerous, whilst there was an unlawful act and there was death, as a bystander watching the events the reasonable man may not foresee the risk of some harm. Flora and her friends had no intent on carrying out any physical attack, they did not chase Angela, and all Angela was doing was running away from the scene.

3 Causes the death of the Victim

The third element of this offence requires proof that the unlawful and dangerous act caused the victim. This aspect of **causation** is vitally important when prosecuting for this offence, it is not enough that the defendant committed an unlawful and dangerous act and the victim died, the two must be linked, the causal chain must be established proving that the unlawful and dangerous act was an operating and substantial cause of the death.

The standard principles of factual and legal causation apply here, including the existing categories of **novus actus interveniens** (discussed in chapter 1).

Key Case
R v Lewis (2010)

Facts: Late one evening a group of students were crossing a road, the defendant in his car had to slow to let them cross and sounded his horn to show his annoyance. The students responded abusively and the defendant got out of the vehicle to confront them. The defendant allegedly punched a female student, her brother (the victim) then intervened to protect her, the brother then ran away from the scene, being allegedly chased by the defendant and was struck and killed by another vehicle. The key question for the jury was did the defendant cause the death of the victim because he was escaping further attack from the defendant at the time he was hit, or was he simply running away unaware he was being chased.

Outcome: Guilty

Legal principle: For causation to be proved it must be factually and legally established that the death was caused by the defendant's unlawful act, this can be proved if the actions of the victim in running away were 'at least one of the responses that may have been expected of some-one in his situation'. This is perfectly acceptable ordinary language to explain the test of objective reasonable foreseeability.

Example: Simone's Vulnerable Victim

Simone burgled the house of an elderly couple that she had been watching for a number of days. She knew they went to bed around 10pm, so she entered the property at 2am knowing they would be asleep by then. As Simone was in the kitchen, Iris, one of the homeowners, came downstairs to get a glass of water and saw Simone in her kitchen. Simone threatened Iris to keep quiet or she would come back and get her in her sleep. Simone left and Iris had a heart attack as a result of her age and the shock of the incident. Iris was dead before paramedics arrived at the scene. It was unlikely that a younger person in this situation would have suffered a heart attack.

Within the context of causation, the thin skull rule would apply to Iris's age and physical condition meaning that the chain of causation is not affected simply because Iris was more susceptible to the heart attack because of her age.

Causation within the context of unlawful act manslaughter provides a unique issue for judicial deliberation, this is when a drug dealer provides a victim with illegal drugs (an unlawful act), but the victim then self-injects those drugs. In these circumstances has the unlawful and dangerous act of drug dealing caused the death? Or has the victim's action of self-injection caused the death, meaning drug dealer avoids prosecution for causing the death.

This particular issue arises within the context of manslaughter rather than murder, as when providing illegal drugs, the drug dealer unlikely has intention to kill or cause GBH, they likely only have intent to deal the drugs, and ultimately would probably want continued custom. The law has developed quite clear principles upon this area.

1. If a defendant injects a victim at their request / with their consent (without intent to kill or cause GBH) they commit an initial unlawful and dangerous act of 'administering a noxious substance' as charged under **s23 Offences against the Persons Act 1861** and may be guilty of unlawful act manslaughter despite the consent of the victim.

Key Case
R v Cato (1976)

Facts: The defendant and victim both drug addicts lived in a house with a number of others, one evening by prior agreement they prepared their own syringes of drugs and then injected each other on a number of occasions. The next morning the victim died as a result of the ingestion of drugs.

Outcome: Guilty

Legal principle: The consent of the victim was immaterial and provides no defence to a defendant, if the defendant's unlawful act of administering a noxious substance contributed to or accelerated the victim's death, then causation is established irrelevant of any preceding consent.

2. If a defendant supplies drugs and even continues to prepare an injection for the victim, if the victim then self-injects, the defendant has not committed a s.23 offence and will not be guilty of unlawful act manslaughter.

Key Case
R v Kennedy (2007)

Facts: The defendant lived in a hostel with others, at the request of the victim the defendant prepared a syringe of heroin and passed it to the victim who self-injected, the victim then passed the syringe back to the defendant who left the room. The victim then died as a consequence of the drug-taking.

Outcome: Not guilty

Legal principle: Whilst it is not disputed that the supply of drugs is an unlawful act, here it is not the unlawful supply of drugs that caused the death. The law recognises the free will of the individual, adults of sound mind make independent decisions, in this case victim made a 'voluntary and informed decision' to inject the drugs. It was the act of self-injection that caused the victim's death, and this broke the causal chain between any actions of the defendant and the death of the victim.

Example: Millie's Spiked Drink

Riley, a well-known drug dealer was in a nightclub one evening with a number of intoxicated women. He spiked the drink of one of the women, Millie and picked up the glass and put it to her mouth to drink. She consumed the drink believing it to contain vodka and coke. Millie later died as a consequence of ingesting the hidden drug.

In these circumstances Riley has committed an offence of administering a noxious substance because he was actively involved in her consumption of it, i.e., he was holding the glass.

Millie's consent would likely not break the chain of causation her because she was only consenting to the drinking of the drink, not to the drugs contained within it, of which she was not aware.

4 Mens rea for the initial unlawful act

The final element of the offence of unlawful act manslaughter requires proof of mens rea. It is a common misconception of the law of homicide that those convicted of manslaughter cause death accidentally and don't require any mental fault. Whilst the offence of unlawful act manslaughter does not require intention to kill or cause GBH, or indeed any foresight of harm to the victim by the defendant (dangerousness is an objective test), it does require proof of mens rea in relation to the initial unlawful and dangerous act. This element is essential to establishing fault on behalf of the defendant, and therefore justifying the imposition of liability for the death.

The initial unlawful and dangerous act must be a complete one, in other words both the actus reus and mens rea of the initial act must be present. This is the only element of mens rea that needs to be proven for unlawful act manslaughter. This means, that if you are familiar with the unlawful act that forms the basis of unlawful act manslaughter, you can outline the mens rea and apply as you usually would with reference to the generic principles of mens rea.

Key Case
DPP v Newbury and Jones (1976)

Facts: Three boys were on a bridge above a trainline, they threw part of a paving stone off of the bridge as a train passed under the bridge, it broke through the train window, hit the guard and caused their death. It was proved that the two defendants in the case jointly pushed the paving stone together. The defendants appealed to the House of Lords upon the basis that they could not be guilty of manslaughter because they did not foresee that their actions could have resulted in harm.

Outcome: Guilty

Legal principle: There is no requirement within the law of unlawful act manslaughter that a defendant can only be convicted if they foresaw the risk of some harm to another. The only element of mens rea that is required is the mens rea of the unlawful act and no more. Further it is not a requirement of the offence or the mens rea to prove that the defendant knew the act was either unlawful or dangerous.

It is also important to note that the principle of **transferred malice** *(discussed in chapter 1)* can apply to this offence, so it is possible for the initial unlawful act to be aimed at one victim, but the death of a different victim be caused. This is in line with the principle established in **R v Larkin (1943)** regarding dangerousness

Key Case
R v Mitchell (1983)

Facts: The defendant pushed an elderly gentleman in a post office queue, the elderly gentlemen (his intended victim) fell onto an elderly woman who suffered a broken leg (his unintended victim), she subsequently died as a consequence of her injuries. The defendant was prosecuted for the offence of unlawful act manslaughter in related to the elderly woman.

Outcome: Guilty

Legal principle: The mens rea was transferred from his intended victim to the additional victim, making him guilty of an offence against the unintended additional victim. He committed an unlawful act (via transferred malice) against the elderly woman which was dangerous given the circumstances and in turn caused her death.

Gross negligence manslaughter

Gross negligence manslaughter is another type of involuntary manslaughter, this means that the defendant has caused the victim's death but did not have the required mens rea to satisfy a murder conviction.

Gross negligence manslaughter is a common law offence, the leading case is **R v Adomako (1994).** In this case Lord Mackay clearly established the four elements of the offence, all of which must be proven in order to establish liability.

Elements of the offence

1. The defendant owes the victim a **duty of care**
2. The defendant **breaches** their duty
3. The breach **causes the death** of the victim
4. The defendant's actions were **grossly negligence** and should be considered criminal

As gross negligence manslaughter is an offence premised upon the tortious concept of negligence, the elements are not clearly broken down into actus reus and mens rea. Whilst there is significant emphasis upon civil law, gross negligence manslaughter is a criminal offence prosecuted online in the criminal courts.

Key Case
R v Adomako (1994)

Facts: The defendant was an anaesthetist who was responsible for the victim during the latter part of an eye operation. During the operation the victim's breathing tube became disconnected and led to cardiac arrest. The defendant failed to notice the disconnection or take appropriate measures to deal with the situation. The standard of care was regarded as 'abysmal' and the defendant admitted negligence, though denied gross negligence.

Outcome: Guilty.

Legal principle: Gross negligence manslaughter is proved by firstly establishing breach of a duty of care, and this is to be established via the ordinary law of negligence. It then must be proved the breach of duty caused the death. Once all of this is proved a jury must then consider if there is evidence of gross negligence and therefore a crime.

Example: Crossover of Offences

There are many circumstances where a defendant could be prosecuted for either manslaughter offence. In the case of R v Willoughby (2005) the following example was given.

'… an employer travelling with an employee driver, whom he has required to deliver goods at high speed, through a built-up area, causing the death of an innocent pedestrian, secondly a doctor who dangerously waives a scalpel, cutting the throat a patient. Both employer and doctor could be guilty of manslaughter by both routes.

1 The defendant owes the victim duty of care

The first element of this manslaughter offence requires that the defendant owes the victim a duty of care, the same duty of care that you would establish in the tort of negligence. As confirmed in **R v Adomako (1994)** this means that there is no separate or alternative test that should be used within this criminal law context to identify a duty of care, when determining if there is a duty of care present for the purposes of gross negligence manslaughter you rely upon the tortious common law principles.

Previously it was thought that in order to identify a duty of care, the three-part test established in **Caparo v Dickman (1990)** should be applied to determine if there was a duty of care present, this understanding was recently corrected in the case of **Robinson v Chief Constable of West Yorkshire (2018).**

Key Case
Robinson v Chief Constable of West Yorkshire (2018)

Facts: Mrs Robinson suffered injuries when she was knocked over and fallen on by two Police Officers who were physically apprehending a suspected drug dealer whilst she was in close physical proximity. Both the trial court and Court of Appeal held that as Police Officers the two were immune from a claim in negligence in line with the existing authority on this point, Hill v Chief Constable of West Yorkshire (1989).

Outcome: Liable

Legal principle: The Caparo test does not have to be strictly applied in every case, instead the courts should look to existing statutes and precedents and identify duties through analogy. Where there is an existing or analogous duty that can be applied, the courts do not need to consider the Caparo test, as such consideration has already been determined, recognising the duty. Only in novel duty situations does this need to be considered.

Additionally, public authorities are subject to the same liabilities in tort law as private individuals. They are under a duty not to cause the public harm via their own actions but are not under a duty to prevent harm from third parties. The Police are not exempt from claims in negligence.

Exam Gold Whilst it is important to correctly outline and apply the duty of care principles it is also important to remember that if you are discussing this offence, you are sitting a criminal law not a tort law exam. Outline the basic concept of duty of care, then identify a duty either through an existing precedent, or explain the incremental approach. Often for gross negligent manslaughter the duty is owed via an omission that has resulted from the defendant failing to act. See Chapter 1 for omission principles and existing precedent that can be applied.

Example: Teddy's Nut Allergy

Aayon, a nursery worker was responsible for preparing the lunch meals for the children in the nursery. On Monday's and Wednesday's Teddy, a 3-year-old boy attended the nursery. Teddy's parents had informed the nursery that Teddy was severely allergic to nuts, to the extent that he would get a reaction if he was in the same rooms as nuts. One Monday, Aayon was tired from the weekend and forgot that Teddy was at the nursery that day. She prepared peanut butter sandwiches for the children, Teddy ate his sandwich and later died from a severe allergic reaction. The nursery called an ambulance and administered his EpiPen but unfortunately, he could not be saved.

Aayon may be guilty of gross negligence manslaughter upon the basis that she owed a duty of care to Teddy as his nursery worker, she breached this by giving him food he was allergic too and this caused his death. It would be up to the jury to determine if they believed this amounted to gross negligence.

Whether there is a duty of care capable of being imposed in a given situation is a matter to be determined by the courts.

> ### Key Case
> ### R v Willoughby (2005)
>
> **Facts:** The defendant owned a disused pub which he owed a large amount of debt on. The defendant recruited the victim to help him set fire to the pub in order to gain insurance monies. In the course of the fire an explosion occurred which led to the premises collapsing and the victim died as a result of the injuries he received. The defendant denied being causing the fire despite a petrol can being found in his car.
>
> **Outcome:** Guilty
>
> **Legal principle:** In this case a duty was not owed solely because the defendant was the owner of premises, but by this fact combined with the fact that he recruited the victim to aid him in this venture for his financial gain. Whether a duty of care is capable of being present in a particular set of circumstances is to be determined by the judge, the actual existence of a duty in each case should then be determined by the jury. Further, there was a duty of care present despite the fact that the two were engaging in a criminal enterprise.

This case therefore not only confirms that who should determine whether a duty of care is present, but further is an authority for the fact that the civil maxim of 'Ex turpi causa' does not apply in criminal cases. This maxim applies in civil cases and means that a criminal cannot make a claim in negligence against their co-conspirator, as demonstrated in **R v Willoughby (2005)** the criminal law is not subject to such a restriction.

> ### Examples of recognised duties
> The law already recognises a wide range of duties, you can draw upon either civil or criminal examples.
>
> **R v Adomako (1994):** medical professionals owe a duty of care to their patients.
>
> **R v Instan (1893):** a duty of care can be imposed where one party assumes responsibility for another.
>
> **R v Gibbins and Proctor (1918):** a duty because of a relationship: generally, only a parent – child relationship will suffice.
>
> **R v Evans (2009):** a duty to act because the defendant has created a dangerous situation: this arises where the defendant sets in a motion a dangerous series of events, where they fails to prevent harm or damage occurring as a result of their actions, this failure to act can form the actus reus of a criminal offence.
>
> **R v Willoughby (2005):** a duty can arise because of a combination of factors.

2 The defendant must have breached his duty

As similar to the tort of negligence, once it has been established that a duty of care is owing from a defendant to a claimant, it must then be further proved that the duty of care was breached by the defendant. Again, **R v Adomako (1994)** confirmed that the ordinary principles of negligence apply when determining if the defendant has breached his duty of care.

The meaning of breach and fundamental nature of negligence, was defined in the case of **Blyth v Birmingham Waterworks co (1865)** where Baron Alderson quoted in his judgment, 'Negligence is the omission to do something which a reasonable man… would do, or doing something which a prudent and reasonable man would not do.'

In accordance with this test, the breach of duty may be proven in one of two ways, either, by doing something that the reasonable man would not have done (via an act) or failing to do something that the reasonable man would have done (an omission). Therefore, negligence can be established via an omission, though it is important to note than an omission does not automatically attract liability, an omission can only satisfy breach if the particular defendant owes the claimant a duty of care at the time of the omission and the omission constituted unreasonable behaviour.

> **Exam Gold** In an application question, similar to your discussion of duty of care, when defining and applying breach it is important not to spend too much time on the civil principles in a criminal exam. Provide a basic definition of breach and apply with reference to the circumstances of the scenario, where the breach is and what the nature of it is. You should not spend any time providing a detailed application upon the type of reasonable man and risk factors like you would in a paper 2 exam.

One aspect of breach of duty which does expand beyond the tortious concept of breach is that for gross negligence manslaughter it must be proved that the breach of duty created a risk of death.

Key Case
R v Rudling (2016)

Facts: The victim (Ryan Morse, aged 12 years) died of a rare autoimmune disease called Addison's disease. The disease was not diagnosed until after his death. Ryan's doctor, Dr Rudling, was prosecuted for gross negligence manslaughter, not because of the failure to accurately diagnose (given the rarity of the condition) but rather because when the victim had been particularly unwell and his mother had spoken with the doctor by phone, due to ongoing illness and the victim's genitals having gone black she requested an urgent visit which the doctor refused and stated it would be due to hormones. The victim died shortly afterwards, it was the prosecution case that if Dr Rudling had visited as requested, she would have sent the victim to hospital immediately for life-saving treatment. Medical evidence suggested that a diagnosis even at the final stages of the disease would have allowed effective treatment and prevented his death.

Outcome: Not guilty

Legal principle: It has long been a principle of gross negligence manslaughter that at the time of the breach it must be reasonably foreseeable that there is a serious and obvious risk of death. In this case at the time of the phone call, which was the breach, there was no serious and obvious risk of death to the defendant. The circumstances of the phone call created a need for a physical examination, but there was no obvious life-threatening condition at the time of the telephone conversation.

Example: Police Officers Duty to Prisoners

Simon was a custody officer at a police station on a night shift, responsible for monitoring vulnerable prisoners. One evening he was watching two prisoners who were known suicide risks. He had been instructed to check on them both every 5 minutes. He became distracted on his phone and didn't check the two inmates for fifteen minutes, during this time one of the vulnerable inmates, Ewan, had taken his own life.

In this scenario a duty of care is owed by the position as custody officer, the breach of failure to monitor does create a risk of death with known suicide risks, this has caused the victim's death by contributing to it, and the conduct could be determined by the jury to be grossly negligent.

---

3 The defendant's breach of duty must have caused the death of the victim

As common with all the homicide offences, for gross negligence manslaughter it must be proved that the defendant **factually and legally caused the death of the victim** (discussed in chapter 1). Within the context of this offence, it must be proved that it is the breach of duty that has caused the death of the victim.

Therefore, when applying factual causation, the courts will consider 'but for the defendant's breach of duty would the victim have died?' Factual causation is only satisfied where it is proved that the death would not have occurred had the defendant fulfilled their duty of care.

Within this context there is also consideration of drugs cases involving self-injection. It has been firmly established within unlawful act manslaughter that if a victim self-injects, this breaks any chain of causation between the defendant's supply of drug and the death of the victim. In the below case the courts were presented with an incredibly sad, but legally interesting case where they had the opportunity to consider how the offence of gross negligence manslaughter operates within this context.

> ## Key Case
> ### R v Evans (2009)
> **Facts:** The victim, a 17 year old heroin addict named Carly, was given heroin by her sister and mother and self-injected whilst residing in their mother's house. It became clear that the victim was suffering from an overdose, but the defendants chose not to seek medical assistance for fear of discovery of the drugs and simply put the victim to bed. The two defendants slept in the same room as the victim. They both awoke the next day to find that the victim had died and were both prosecuted for gross negligence manslaughter.
>
> **Outcome:** Guilty
>
> **Legal principle:** There were no issues of causation in the case. The self-injection of the victim arose before the breach of duty. The duty arose as the mother and sister were concerned in the supply of heroin and subsequently realised that the situation had become life-threatening, once it was clear that the state of affairs was life-threatening the breach was failure to take reasonable steps to ensure the safety of the victim.

4 It must be proved that the negligence (the defendant's breach of duty) was gross

The final element of this offence is one that clearly distinguishes gross negligence manslaughter as a criminal offence from the civil tort of negligence. Gross negligence requires proof of a much higher standard of fault than the civil standard of negligence and it is the severity of this element that justifies the introduction of civil principles into the criminal courts.

Under the civil law negligence is proved simply by falling below the expected standard of care, the extent to which the defendant must have departed from the usual standards is not specified. Within gross negligence manslaughter a specific standard of departure from the expected standards must be proved.

In **R v Adomako (1994)** it was held 'the essence of the matter which is supremely a jury question is whether having regard to the risk of death involved, the conduct of the defendant was so bad in all the circumstances as to amount in their judgment to a criminal act or omission'.

> ### Example: Perdetta's drug addiction
> Perdetta was a pharmacist who was, unknown to her colleagues, addicted to prescription painkillers. She tried to avoid taking them at work as they caused her to suffer from blurred vision, confusion and at worst to hallucinate. One Friday morning, she took a dose of painkillers at work and continued dispensing medications. A patient needed 10mg tablets of a medicine and due to blurred vision, Perdetta was unable to see properly, she mistakenly dispensed 100mg tablets. The patient was visually impaired so unable to check these. Perdetta didn't ask a colleague to check the prescription and gave them to the patient. The patient died from the overdose of medication.
>
> A jury may well conclude that Perdetta is grossly negligent here, being under the influence of drugs whilst undertaking a role with such responsibility could be considered so bad in all the circumstances.

Key Terms – Fatal Offences Against the Person - Involuntary Manslaughter

Manslaughter	The killing of one human being by another, unlawfully, but without the required mens rea for murder
Unlawful act manslaughter	A defendant will be convicted of unlawful act manslaughter where they commit an initial unlawful and dangerous act (separate criminal offence) which causes the death of the victim.
Initial unlawful act	In order for an offence of unlawful act manslaughter to be proved it must firstly be proved that the defendant had the actus reus and mens rea of a separate, initial unlawful act.
Dangerousness	The initial unlawful act must be proved to be objectively dangerous; this means the reasonable man as a bystander to the events would have foreseen the risk of harm occurring as a consequence of the acts.
Reasonable bystander	When determining dangerousness objectively, the test operates as if the reasonable man is a bystander to the events and has the knowledge of the defendant and no more.

Key Terms – Fatal Offences Against the Person - Involuntary Manslaughter

Gross negligence manslaughter	An offence premised upon the basis that a defendant breaches a duty of care owing to the victim, which causes their death, and the breach is deemed grossly negligent.
Duty of care	A duty to take reasonable steps to prevent the causing of harm to another imposed by law.
Breach of duty	A failure to meet the standard of care required by the reasonable man in the circumstances, for the offence of gross negligence manslaughter this must create a risk of death.
Risk of death	It must be proved for this offence that the breach of duty created a reasonably foreseeable serious and obvious risk of death.
Gross negligence	A higher standard of negligence than the tortious standard of negligence, requires proof that the defendant

One Sentence Case Summary – Fatal Offences Against the Person - Involuntary Manslaughter – Unlawful Act Manslaughter

Name	Topic Link	Legal significance
R v Lamb (1967)	UAM – Initial unlawful act	In order for UAM to be proved the technical requirements of an initial and separate offence must be proved, namely the actus reus and mens rea.
R v Andrews (1937)	UAM – Initial unlawful act	Negligent acts that would usually constitute civil liability cannot satisfy an offence of unlawful act manslaughter.
R v Farnon and Ellis (2015)	UAM – Initial unlawful act	Prosecutions for UAM can proceed upon the basis of any criminal offence, relevant initial unlawful acts are not limited to offences against the person, in this case the initial unlawful act was arson, an offence against property.
R v Church (1966)	UAM – dangerousness	An initial unlawful act is dangerous if the reasonable man would recognise that it subjects another person to the risk of some harm.
R v Dawson (1985)	UAM – dangerousness	When determining dangerousness objectively, the test should be considered as if the reasonable man was watching the unlawful act be performed with the knowledge of the defendant and nothing more, unknown factors or circumstances cannot be considered within the determination of dangerousness.
R v Farnon and Ellis (2015)	UAM – dangerousness	When determining dangerousness, the test is entirely objective, there is no subjective consideration of the age or mental capacity of the defendants when determining if the defendants would have foreseen the risk of some harm.
R v JM and another (2012)	UAM – dangerousness	The test of dangerousness does not demand that the reasonable man must foresee that type of physical harm from which the victim ultimately dies, it is enough that they foresee the risk of some physical harm occurring from the unlawful act.
R v Cato (1976)	UAM – Causation – Administration of a noxious substance	Where a defendant injects a defendant at their request or with their consent, this does not act as a defence nor break the causal chain between the administration of the noxious substance and death.
R v Kennedy (2007)	UAM – Causation – Self-injection	Where a defendant supplies drug to a victim who self-injects, the supply of drugs is not the cause of death, but instead the voluntary and informed decision of the victim to self-inject is the recognised legal cause.

One Sentence Case Summary – Fatal Offences Against the Person - Involuntary Manslaughter – Unlawful Act Manslaughter

Name	Topic Link	Legal significance
DPP v Newbury and Jones (1976)	UAM – Mens rea	There is no requirement within the law of unlawful act manslaughter that a defendant can only be convicted if they foresaw the risk of some harm to another, only the mens rea of the initial unlawful act need be proved.
R v Mitchell (1983)	UAM – Mens rea – transferred malice	The principle of transferred malice can operate for the offence of unlawful act manslaughter meaning that a defendant can be convicted where an unintended victim dies as a result of an unlawful act against an intended victim.

One Sentence Case Summary – Fatal Offences Against the Person - Involuntary Manslaughter – Gross negligence Manslaughter

Name	Topic Link	Legal significance
R v Adomako (1994)	GNM – Leading case	The leading case for gross negligence manslaughter, the four elements of liability where clearly established, duty and breach to be established according to the ordinary principles of negligence, further medical professionals owe a duty of care to their patients
Robinson v Chief Constable of West Yorkshire Police (2018)	GNM – Duty of care	This case established that the Caparo test only needs applying in new and novel cases and that the courts should generally establish a duty by looking at existing duty situations and ones with clear analogy.
R v Instan (1893)	GNM – Pre-existing duty of care	A duty of care can be imposed where one party assumes responsibility for another.
R v Gibbins and Proctor (1918)	GNM – Pre-existing duty of care	A duty of care can be imposed because of a relationship: generally, only a parent – child relationship will suffice.
R v Evans (2009)	GNM – Pre-existing duty of care	A duty of care can be imposed because the defendant has created a dangerous situation: this arises where the defendant sets in a motion a dangerous series of events.
R v Willoughby (2005)	GNM – Duty of care	Whether a duty of care is capable of existence is a matter for the judge, in an individual case whether such a duty is present should be determined by the jury. A duty of care can arise because of a combination of factors. A defendant is not immune from prosecution for gross negligence manslaughter because they were acting in the course of a criminal act with the victim as an accomplice, a duty of care can be imposed in these circumstances.
Blyth v Birmingham Waterworks co (1865)	Breach of duty - definition	'Negligence is the omission to do something which a reasonable man, guided upon those considerations which ordinarily regulate the conduct of human affairs, would do, or doing something which a prudent and reasonable man would not do.'

One Sentence Case Summary – Fatal Offences Against the Person - Involuntary Manslaughter – Gross negligence Manslaughter		
Name	**Topic Link**	**Legal significance**
R v Rudling (2016)	Breach of duty – risk of death	For gross negligence manslaughter it must be proved that at the time of the breach there was a reasonably foreseeable risk of death, a serious and obvious risk.
R v Evans (2009)	GNM – Causation	In the law of gross negligence where self-injection occurs prior to the defendant's breach of a pre-existing duty of care, the self-injection has no affect upon the causal chain.
R v Adomako (1994)	GNM – Gross negligence	'The essence of the matter which is supremely a jury question is whether having regard to the risk of death involved, the conduct of the defendant was so bad in all the circumstances as to amount in their judgment to a criminal act or omission'.

NON-FATAL OFFENCES AGAINST THE PERSON

Exam Reference:	H418/01 – The Legal System and Criminal Law (Paper 1)
	Non-fatal offences against the person are substantive topics that appear in paper 1 of the OCR Law A-Level exam series. 60 marks out of 80 are allocated to substantive law topics in this paper. You will be required to accurately identify and explain (AO1) the law on non-fatal offences against the person and apply them to scenario-based situations (AO2). This topic can also feature as the evaluation question where you will be required to analyse and evaluate the law on non-fatal offences against the person (AO3).'
Topic Content:	• Common assault: assault and battery.
	• Offences Against the Person Act 1861: s47 assault/battery occasioning actual bodily harm
	• s20 unlawful and malicious wounding or inflicting grievous bodily harm
	• s18 unlawful and malicious wounding or causing grievous bodily harm with intent to cause grievous bodily harm.

Topic introduction

Non-fatal offences against the person refers to a range of offences which do not result in the death of the victim. Law A Level requires consideration of five offences, but in practice the range of non-fatal offences against the person extends well beyond this. The topic of non-fatal offences against the person is broad, and ranges from behaviour of non-physical contact, to causing serious, even life-threatening harm.

> **Exam Gold** In an application question, one of the challenges can be identifying which non-fatal offence against the person is the correct one, there are a number of strategies that you can use to determine which offence is the most appropriate. For example, if there is shouting but no contact, assault will be the relevant offence. If there is contact (touching) but no harm, then battery will be the correct offence for consideration.

Assault

The offence of assault is under **s39 of the Criminal Justice Act 1998**, it is this section that criminalises the offence and establishes the maximum sentence of 6 months imprisonment. This section however contains no definition of the offence, the substance of the offence and generic principles of liability have alternatively been established by the common law.

It is important to understand how the term assault is used in different contexts, assault is a criminal offence premised upon the basis of causing a victim to apprehend force. The word assault in practice gets used in a number of different contexts which can cause confusion, many other non-fatal offences are sometimes called assaults, further the phrase 'common assault' is used which means assault and / or battery, even further confusing is the phrase 'assault by beating' which is commonly used to describe a battery. So, it is important to exercise caution when researching assault, ensure you are looking at the correct offence.

Elements of the offence

Actus reus	Mens rea
Defendant does an act that **causes the victim to apprehend the infliction of immediate, unlawful force.**	**Intention or recklessness to cause the victim to apprehend immediate unlawful force.**

Actus reus

The actus reus of assault is: The defendant does an act that causes the victim to apprehend the infliction of immediate, unlawful force.

Key Case
Collins v Wilcock (1984)

Facts: The defendant and a friend were suspected of soliciting men for the purposes of prostitution whilst being watched by two police officers. The defendant refused to talk the police officer when approached, so one of the police officers (the victim) took the defendant by the arm, to which the defendant responded by scratching the victim's arm with her fingernails. The defendant was prosecuted for assaulting a police officer in execution of their duty, the defendant claimed the police officer was not executing her lawful duty as she had no right to restrain her then as she was not under arrest.

Outcome: Not guilty

Legal principle: Whilst this case was in fact one of battery, the court confirmed the actus reus of assault to confirm how distinct to battery as 'An assault is an act which causes another person to apprehend the infliction of immediate, unlawful, force on his person'.

Exam Gold In order to effectively use the law of non-fatal offences against the person in the exam you must explain the actus reus and apply by discussing the facts of the scenario. Higher level answers will break down the elements of the actus reus and discuss these separately.

An Act

The phrase 'act' indicates that a defendant cannot commit an assault by omission. A physical action must be undertaken by the defendant in order for the actus reus to be proved. The term 'act' is broad and covers a range of verbal and non-verbal actions.

Examples of assault

There are many actions that could satisfy the actus reus of assault. Some examples include:

- A verbal threat
- A non-verbal gesture e.g., finger across the throat or a making a fist
- Chasing another
- An intimidating glare at another
- A threat of force via letter, e-mail or text message
- A social media post threatening the victim
- Prank phone calls, including silent calls
- Throwing an item at another but missing
- Spitting at another but missing

Key Case
Tuberville v Savage (1669)

Facts: The defendant and victim became involved in a physical altercation, the defendant put his hand on his sword and said, 'If it were not assize time, I would not take such language from you', indicating that if the assize judges were not in town, he would use his sword against the victim. The case questioned whether there was still an assault via the act of grabbing the sword because the defendant declared he was not going to use it.

Outcome: Not guilty

Legal principle: There is no assault where the defendant declares to the victim, they are not going to carry out a threat against them. Words can negate the actus reus of an assault.

Silence can also amount to an assault.

> ## Key Case
> ### R v Ireland (1997)
>
> **Facts:** The defendant made a number of silent phone calls to three different women over the course of three months. He did not speak for the duration of the calls and would breathe heavily down the line. As a result of the calls the women suffered psychiatric harm. Defendant appealed his conviction on the basis that silence could not amount to an assault (and that psychiatric harm was not assault occasioning actual bodily harm.)
>
> **Outcome:** Guilty of assault occasioning actual bodily harm
>
> **Legal principle:** Lord Steyn confirmed that silent phone calls can constitute an assault where it causes the victim to apprehend fear. Proximity of the defendant and victim is irrelevant, fear can be induced over the telephone. Additionally silent calls leading to psychiatric injury can amount to s47 actual bodily harm.

Apprehension

Once it has been proved that an act is present it must be proved that the victim apprehended force as a consequence of that act, this means that they expected or anticipated force from the defendant against themselves.

Apprehension is what turns an act into an assault, the performance of an act alone does not establish an assault, there is only an assault if the act performed by the defendant does cause an expectation of force for the victim, and further the mens rea requires that by that act the defendant intended or was reckless as to causing that apprehension.

Even if a defendant intends to cause apprehension of force by their acts, if this is not caused to the victim, the actus reus of assault is not satisfied.

> ## Key Case
> ### R v Logdon (1976)
>
> **Facts:** The defendant pointed a replica gun at the victim in gest, not intending to frighten them. Upon realisation that the victim was indeed fearful that the gun was real, the defendant told the victim it was a replica and that they were at no danger of harm.
>
> **Outcome:** Guilty
>
> **Legal principle:** A defendant may be guilty of assault despite the fact that they did not have the means, nor intent of carrying out any threat. Whilst he did not necessarily intend to cause her apprehension, there was at least recklessness as to this occurring.

> **Example: Melissa's Unheard Threat**
>
> Melissa was a part of a gang who lived on an estate, which was notorious for harassing the other residents. They would often vandalise cars, spray graffiti on house fronts and generally be abusive towards the residents.
>
> One day Enid, an elderly lady, was walking past Melissa and her friends, when Melissa deliberately started talking very loudly saying *'I think I want to do over an old lady's house soon and break all their antique rubbish they keep in their house, might rough them up a bit too'*.
>
> Enid happened to not hear this because she did not have her hearing aids in. Whilst the words of Melissa are more than capable of amounting to an assault, if there is no apprehension (fear) caused, there is no assault.

Immediacy

The actus reus of assault not only demands that the defendant caused the victim to apprehend force via their act, but that the victim apprehended that the force was going to be immediate. This means that the victim anticipates that the force is going to be used against them within a very short timeframe. The courts have been liberal in their interpretation of this, and still found an assault even though force may not be able to be used at that exact moment, there may still be an assault even though the defendant would still need to take further steps before they could execute any kind of threat.

Key Case
Smith v Chief Constable of Woking Police Station (1983)

Facts: One evening the defendant entered the victim's enclosed garden and looked through the window of the victim's bedroom, the victim noticed the defendant in her garden directly outside her window, watching her, and was terrified at his presence, fearful as to why he was in her garden and that he may try and hurt her.

Outcome: Guilty

Legal principle: Despite the fact that at the time of the offence she may not have been able to articulate exactly what she was terrified of, and despite the fact that he was outside of the window so could not have harmed her in that instant, this could still amount to an assault. There was apprehension upon the basis that she did not know what he was going to do next but feared that it was violent.

Mens rea

The mens rea of assault is 'intention to cause the victim to apprehend immediate unlawful force or recklessness as to whether such apprehension is caused'.

Exam Gold Where an offence can be satisfied by either intention or recklessness, in an application question you only need to identify and apply one of these types of mens rea. In addition, because the offence can be satisfied by recklessness, it is not necessary to consider the law of indirect intention.

Battery

Battery is a non-fatal offence against the person premised upon the application of force, this is also what makes it distinct from assault, assault is a non-contact-based offence, battery is a contact-based offence.

Elements of the offence:

Actus reus	Mens rea
The **infliction of unlawful force on another person.**	Intention or recklessness to apply unlawful force to another.

Actus reus

The actus reus of battery is: the actual infliction of unlawful force on another person.

Key Case
Collins v Wilcock (1984)

Facts: The defendant and a friend were suspected of soliciting men for the purposes of prostitution whilst being watched by two police officers. The defendant refused to talk the police officer when approached, so the police officer (the victim) took the defendant by the arm, to which the defendant responded by scratching the victim's arm with her fingernails. The defendant was prosecuted for assaulting a police officer in execution of their duty, the defendant claimed the police officer was not executing her lawful duty as she had no right to restrain her then as she was not under arrest.

Outcome: Not guilty

Legal principle: The court confirmed the actus reus of battery as 'the actual infliction of unlawful force on another person'. Further, it was held that there was no battery here as she was using lawful force to defend herself from an offence against the police officer.

Examples of battery

There are many actions that could satisfy the actus reus of battery. Some examples include:
- **Pushing**
- **Grabbing**
- **Touching but leaving no injury**
- **Unwanted tickling**
- **Touching clothing whilst that person is wearing it**
- **Throwing an item at another including throwing fluid (such as a drink) onto someone**
- **Spitting on another**

Infliction

The offence of battery requires proof that the defendant has actually inflicted force on the victim, the law has developed to find that this can be committed directly or indirectly.

Key Case
Haystead v Chief Constable of Derbyshire (2000)

Facts: A woman had been involved in a relationship with the defendant, she had a young son of 12 months old from a previous relationship. The woman sought to end the relationship with the defendant, as a result of which he threatened her. One evening he came to her home and punched her twice in the face whilst she was holding her son, as a result the child fell to the floor and hit his head. The defendant denied the offence of battery to the child as he applied no force directly to him and nor did he have any intent to hurt the child.

Outcome: Guilty

Legal principle: There was an offence of battery to the child in this case, battery is not limited to the direct application of violence, force can be applied indirectly.

Unlawful

The actus reus of battery is essentially the unlawful touching of another, touching of others is something that we do in our everyday lives, and sometimes without realising, or by accident. This does not mean that every time we touch another person, we are committing this non-fatal offence against the person. Key to the actus reus of battery is that the application for force is unlawful. The majority of force that is applied in everyday life is lawful and therefore not within the remit of this offence.

> **Example: Collins v Wilcock**
>
> In **Collins v Wilcock (1984)** the court gave many examples of when the use of force was consensual, and thus lawful and would not amount to a battery. Examples of where the use of force was lawful included:
> - Force applied in the course of lawful arrest
> - Force applied in self-defence
> - Force applied in ordinary physical contacts of everyday life – by moving within society there is an implied consent E.g., whilst in a supermarket, underground station or in the course of a handshake used as a greeting
> - Force applied when tapping a person to get their attention
> - actus reus of battery is: the actual infliction of unlawful force on another person.

Key Case
Wilson v Pringle (1986)

Facts: The defendant (a 12 year old schoolboy), intentionally pulled the bag of the victim (also a 12 year old schoolboy) in the school yard, causing the victim to suffer injury to his hip. The defendant argued it was ordinary horseplay. The victim argued it was an intentional battery.

Outcome: Liable. This was a Tort case (trespass against the person amounting to battery) which considered the principles of what constitutes a battery.

Legal principle: The court confirmed that battery must be intentional and hostile touching. Also confirmed that acting in self-defence would amount to lawful touching.

Force

The actus reus of battery is premised upon the basis that force has been applied to the victim. By the fact that if any harm was caused, battery is no longer the appropriate offence, we can logically conclude that the level of force for this offence does not need to be significant.

In the case of **Collins v Wilcock (1984)** it was held that 'It has long been established that any touching of another person, however slight, may amount to a battery'.

This establishes that a very low level of force will satisfy the actus reus of battery.

Key Case
R v Thomas (1985)

Facts: The defendant (a school caretaker) touched and rubbed the hem of two schoolgirl's skirts (the victims, aged 11 and 12 years.) The jury had acquitted the caretaker on 10 other similar counts.

Outcome: Guilty

Legal principle: The judge clarified that touching a person's clothing, whilst that person is wearing them, is equivalent to touching the person.

> **Example: Water Balloon Prank**
>
> Connor, a 12 year old schoolboy, loved playing pranks on teachers and students alike. One day he left 10 full water balloons hanging above the staff room door, which would drop on the next person who walked through them. Mr Fletcher, the Geography teacher, walked through the door and the balloons dropped on him and popped, no harm was caused to him.
>
> Being hit by the balloons would be the application of force, which he did not expressly or impliedly consent to and would amount to battery. Whilst it was only meant as a harmless prank, Connor intended a teacher to get hit by the balloons, which is intention to apply unlawful force.

Mens rea

The mens rea of battery is intention to apply unlawful force to another or recklessness as to whether such force is applied. *Assault and battery are distinct from the remaining three offences as they do not require any proof of harm in order to establish conviction.*

> **Exam Gold** In an application question, if the defendant makes contact with the victim but causes no harm, this would indicate to you to discuss the offence of battery. If the scenario facts give any suggestion of harm, you should consider battery but also discuss in addition the possibility of that amounting to actual bodily harm.

Assault occasioning actual bodily harm

Assault occasioning actual bodily harm is the first of three non-fatal offences against the person that are dependent upon proving that the defendant caused a certain level of harm to the victim. The offence is charged under **s47 Offences against the Persons Act 1861** which specifies the maximum sentence of 5 years imprisonment. This section however does little to define or elaborate upon the nature of the offence, so these principles have been established by the common law.

Elements of the offence:

Actus reus	Mens rea
The defendant commits an **assault or battery occasioning actual bodily harm**.	The defendant **has intention or recklessness to the initial assault or battery**.

Actus reus

There are three distinct aspects to the actus reus of this offence, each must be proved for the offence to be complete.

Assault

Within the context of s.47 this means 'common assault', for this offence it must be proved that the defendant committed an initial assault **or** an initial battery, in the exam you must clearly identify which is present.

> **Example: Frankie the Bully**
>
> Mika's younger sister Edie, had been bullied by Frankie for a number of years. Mika was at the park one day when he saw Frankie with her friends, Mika wanted to scare Frankie to stop her bullying Edie and immediately ran at Frankie shouting 'If I get hold of you, I am going to make you pay for what you have done'. Frankie then started running away from Mika who continued chasing her. Frankie fell on uneven ground and hit her face, causing her front two teeth to be broken.
>
> This is an example of an assault occasioning actual bodily harm. The assault is by words / chasing, and this caused the actual bodily harm as the running away from the threat is a reasonably foreseeable act of the victim. Broken teeth would likely be regarded as actual bodily harm, as whilst evident harm, it is not serious so would not move the offence to one of grievous bodily harm.

Occasioning

This aspect of the actus reus requires you to establish causation, both factual and legal and apply the relevant cases. You are trying to prove an unbroken chain of causation between the initial assault or battery and the actual bodily harm suffered by the victim. It is not sufficient that there was an assault or battery by the defendant and the victim separately suffered actual bodily harm, there must be a causal link between the two. Factually it must be proved that the actual bodily harm would not have occurred but for the initial assault or battery, and further it must be established that the assault or battery is an operating and substantial cause of the actual bodily harm by establishing an unbroken chain of causation. The standard principles of causation, and possible novus actus interveniens are all applicable to this offence.

Actual bodily harm

Actual bodily harm was not defined within the statute, the term has therefore been developed by the common law. Actual bodily harm has been interpreted by judges to include where the victim has suffered physical and psychiatric injury.

Examples of ABH
There are many actions that could satisfy the actus reus of ABH. Some examples include:
- Bruises
- Scratches and grazes
- Minor sprains and fractures
- A broken nose (as the nose is constructed of cartilage and not bone)
- Broken teeth
- Temporary loss of consciousness
- Psychiatric injury

Key Case
R v Abbas (2009)

Facts: The defendant barged into a group of people outside of a bar, following a brief argument he punched one of the group. The victim fell and hit his head and suffered cuts, bruises and a temporary loss of consciousness.

Outcome: Guilty

Legal principle: Loss of consciousness is evidence of harm sufficient to amount to actual bodily harm.

Key Case
R v Donovan (1934)

Facts: The defendant convinced a 17-year-old girl to go to a garage with him where he indecently assaulted her by beating her with a cane in line with his sexual desires. The defendant denied that any offence took place upon the basis that she consented.

Outcome: Conviction quashed at appeal due to misdirection at trial

Legal principle: A person subject to unlawful acts cannot consent to them as a defence, although some exceptions do exist. The phrase bodily harm is a phrase that should take its ordinary meaning, it 'includes any hurt or injury calculated to interfere with the health or comfort' of the victim. Further 'Such hurt or injury need not be permanent, but must, no doubt, be more than merely transient and trifling'.

Key Case
R v Chan Fook (1994)

Facts: The victim was a French student lodging in the home of an English family. The homeowner's engagement ring went missing and the victim, without evidence was suspected. The homeowner and her partner searched his room but did not find the ring. Her partner then allegedly subjected the victim to a physical assault and locked him in his room, fearful of a continued attack the victim escaped via the bedroom window. As a result, he fell and suffered a range of injuries including a fractured wrist and dislocated pelvis. The prosecution sought their case upon the basis of psychological harm that had been caused to the victim as a result of the whole incident, that he had felt abused and frightened.

Outcome: Not guilty

Legal principle: Actual bodily harm is not limited to physical injuries of the flesh and body, it can include injury in a psychiatric form, however 'it does not include mere emotions such as fear or distress nor panic, as such, states of mind that are not themselves evidence of some identifiable clinical condition'.

Key Case
R v Ireland (1997)

Facts: The defendant made a number of silent phone calls to three different women over the course of three months. He did not speak for the duration of the calls and would breathe heavily down the line. As a result of the calls the women suffered psychiatric harm. Defendant appealed his conviction on the basis that psychiatric harm was not assault occasioning actual bodily harm (and that silence could not amount to an assault.)

Outcome: Guilty of assault occasioning actual bodily harm

Legal principle: Lord Steyn confirmed that the silent calls leading to psychiatric injury can amount to s47 actual bodily harm. The term 'bodily' in s47, s20 and s18 offences against the persons act 1861 is interpreted to include psychiatric injury. The case also confirmed that silent phone calls can constitute an assault where it causes the victim to apprehend fear. Proximity of the defendant and victim is irrelevant, fear can be induced over the telephone.

Key Case
R v D (2006)

Facts: Over a number of years the victim was physically, but mainly psychologically abused by her husband, the defendant. This eventually led to her committing suicide by hanging. On the evening of her death the two had argued and the defendant had physically assaulted her. Medical evidence confirmed that she was suffering from psychological injury at the time of her death as a result of the abuse, although a diagnosis of an established condition could not be proven. The question to be determined was could psychological injury, without having met the threshold of a clinically diagnosed condition, amount to actual bodily harm or grievous bodily harm?

Outcome: Not guilty

Legal principle: Psychological injury cannot amount to bodily harm for the purposes of non-fatal offences against the person, it must be proved that there is a recognisable psychiatric illness.

Exam Gold In an application question if there is some reference to the mental state of the victim after the incident with the defendant this indicates that you should discuss the possibility of psychiatric harm. If, however it just states that a victim felt upset or scared, this may indicate that there is not enough evidence to establish actual bodily harm, but you should still discuss this. If the scenario outlines symptoms that would indicate an identifiable clinical condition e.g., panic, shock, stress etc you should explain and apply the relevant authorities. The examiners are not expecting you to make a formal medical diagnosis, so recognising that this may be enough to satisfy ABH if it is a psychiatric condition rather than just emotions or distress will be sufficient.'

Mens rea

The mens rea of s.47 is often the element that causes the most confusion. For the offences of assault and battery you must prove intention or recklessness in relation to the actus reus, which presents a certain element of logic. However, it is important to note that for a section 47 offence the mens rea is **not** intention or recklessness as to causing actual bodily harm, in fact for this offence the defendant does not have to have any level of foresight in relation to the actual bodily harm at all. In this sense there is some disconnect between the level of harm that has to be proved for the actus reus and level of foresight that has to be proved for the mens rea.

The mens rea of a s47 offence is further complicated because the required mens rea will change according to how the offence is committed. The mens rea of a s47 offence is the mens rea of the initial assault or battery alone. If you have proven an assault occasioning actual bodily harm, you outline and apply the mens rea of assault. If you have proved a battery occasioning actual bodily harm, you outline and apply the mens rea of battery.

The defendant does not need to intend or been reckless as to the actual bodily harm. There is no defence to a defendant to say they had no foresight of the actual bodily harm at all. This was confirmed in the case of **DPP v Parmenter (1992)**.

S.20 Grievous bodily harm or wounding

The next non-fatal offence against the person is contained within **s.20 of the Offences against the Persons Act 1861**, an offence that carries a maximum sentence of five years imprisonment. Again, the aged statute gives very little indication about the nature of the offence and what must be proved, thus we look to the common law to establish these boundaries for practice.

Elements of the offence

Actus reus	Mens rea
The defendant **unlawfully and maliciously wounds or inflicts grievous bodily harm to another**	The defendant **intends or is reckless as to some harm to another**

S. 20 Actus reus

The actus reus of this section can be satisfied if one of two ways, similar to how a s47 offence can be satisfied by either an initial assault or battery. A section 20 offence can be satisfied by proof that the defendant has caused the victim grievous bodily harm, or a wound. It is not necessary that both may be proved, however it may be the case that both are present within one charge.

Grievous bodily harm

This phrase refers to a level of physical or psychiatric harm that must be suffered by the victim, a level of harm more serious than that of actual bodily harm, the s.47 offence.

Examples of GBH

There are many actions that could satisfy the actus reus of GBH. Some examples include:
- **Broken bones**
- **Stab wounds**
- **Bullet wounds**
- **Permanent injuries such as brain damage or disability**
- **Internal bleeding**
- **Loss of limb/s**
- **Psychiatric conditions**

Key Case
R v Saunders (1985)

Facts: Late at night the defendant and victim became involved in an argument and the defendant punched the victim in the face. The punch caused a number of serious injuries.

Outcome: Guilty

Legal principle: Grievous bodily harm requires proof of 'serious injury', it is not necessary for the word 'really' to precede the phrase serious injury.

This can include the transmission of biological and sexually transmitted diseases.

> ### Key Case
> ### R v Dica (2004)
>
> **Facts:** The defendant (Mohammed Dica) was HIV positive. He had unprotected, consensual sexual intercourse with two women who were unaware of his infection. Both women contracted HIV.
>
> **Outcome:** Guilty
>
> **Legal principle:** Knowingly or recklessly transmitting a serious sexual disease to a person who the risk is concealed is equal to s20 grievous bodily harm. If, however, the victim is aware of the risk and consents to this risk consent will provide a defence.

Confirmed in:

> ### Key Case
> ### R v Golding (2014)
>
> **Facts:** The defendant and victim had been in a sexual relationship after which the victim contracted herpes. The defendant admitted that he had infected her with herpes, a condition that he knew he suffered from. The defendant said that he had not intended for her to catch herpes by engaging in sexual intercourse with her but was aware there was a risk she may contract it. The defence denied that herpes was sufficient to amount to serious harm for the purpose of a s20 conviction.
>
> **Outcome:** Guilty
>
> **Legal principle:** Recklessly infecting another with a sexual disease may be guilty of a s20 offence, it is not necessary that the harm to be permanent, dangerous or even require treatment for this offence to be proved. Whether injury is sufficient to amount to grievous bodily harm is a matter for the jury to decide.

The age and health of the victim can be taken into consideration when determining whether the injuries constituted serious harm.

> ### Key Case
> ### R v Bollom (2004)
>
> **Facts:** The grandmother of a 17 month baby took the child to hospital where they were found to have non-accidental bruising and abrasions, the partner of the mother of the child was prosecuted for s18 GBH but denied that the injuries could amount to grievous bodily harm.
>
> **Outcome:** Conviction substituted for one of s.47 ABH.
>
> **Legal principle:** When determining if injuries amount to serious harm, the particulars of the victim should be considered, this may involve reference to their age, health and effect of the harm upon the individual victim. Given reference to the individual and the number of bruises it was acceptable of the jury to conclude that this amounted to grievous bodily harm, when reviewing the injuries, they should be considered in their totality rather than individually.

> **Exam Gold** In an application question where the actions of the defendant have caused harm to the defendant but not death, the first thing to consider is whether the injuries amount to actual bodily harm or grievous bodily harm. The first question to ask yourself is are the injuries that the victim has suffered serious? In determining this you should consider the impact of the injuries on the victim, the level of pain they have experienced, the permanence of the injuries, the treatment required and overall effect on their lifestyle.

Wound

An alternative way that the actus reus of s.20 can be satisfied is via proof of a wound. In some circumstances if the nature of the wound is severe enough it may also be regarded as grievous bodily harm.

> ### Key Case
> ### JJC v Eisenhower (1984)
>
> **Facts:** Two 15-year-old boys purchased an air pistol and pellets, one afternoon the shot across a road at a group of people and hit the victim in the left eye. The pellet caused bruising around the eye and fluid to fill within the eye likely caused by the internal rupture of blood vessels.
>
> **Outcome:** Not guilty of wounding
>
> **Legal principle:** for a wound to be proved there must be a 'break in the continuity of the whole of the skin', this means both the outer and under layers of the skin. Internal bleeding which is caused by breaking of an internal layer of skin is not a wound as the whole of the skin has not been broken.

Causation

Having established that the victim has suffered a level of harm or a wound sufficient to amount to a s20 offence, you must establish that the defendant has caused this via the ordinary principles of factual and legal causation.

Unlike a s47 offence it does not have to be proved that the grievous bodily harm or wounding was caused by an initial assault or battery, simply that it was caused by the actions of the defendant.

S.20 Mens Rea

The mens rea of s20, similar to a s47 offence does not require intention or recklessness in relation to the actus reus (causing of GBH or a wound). The mens rea instead requires a lower level of foresight, foresight of 'some harm'.

The mens rea of section 20 was confirmed in the case of **DPP v Parmenter (1992)** as intention or recklessness as to some harm. This means that whilst for the actus reus you have to prove serious harm, or a wound, the mens rea only requires foresight or intention of some harm, a subtle but important difference.

> #### Example: Aran's Attack
>
> Aran was in the queue for a nightclub when a group of men behind him, who were drunk, started becoming racially abusive towards him. Aran, who had also consumed a considerable amount of alcohol, turned around and warned them to stop or ' he would make them stop'. Gary laughed at Aran's threats, started pushing Aran and continued to make racist remarks. Aran reacted by punching Gary, causing bleeding and significant bruising. Gary suffered a bleed on the brain and had to spend two weeks in intensive care before making a full recovery.
>
> This would likely be prosecuted as a s20 offence rather than s18. Whilst Aran carried out the attack, he did not initiate the conflict, it was not pre-meditated, he did not use a weapon and intention to cause 'serious harm' is unclear. All of these factors suggest that s20 may be the correct offence to prosecute rather than s18 as intention or recklessness as to 'some' harm would be easier to prove here.

S18 Grievous bodily harm or wounding with intent

The final non-fatal offence for consideration here is the offence of GBH or wounding with intent. This offence is contained within **s.18 of the Offences against the Persons Act 1861** and the maximum sentence is life imprisonment.

This offence is a much more serious offence than s20, as indicated by the maximum available sentence. Whilst the actus reus of s18 is exactly the same as a s20 offence it has a different level of foresight required for the mens rea. It is this difference, and this difference alone that establishes a higher level of culpability and justifies the significantly increased possibly maximum sentence.

Elements of the offence:

Actus reus	Mens rea
The defendant **maliciously wounds or causes grievous bodily harm on another**	The defendant **intends grievous bodily harm or intends to resist lawful arrest**

S.18 Actus reus

The actus reus of s.18 is exactly the same as s.20, it can be satisfied by proof of either serious harm identified as GBH, or a wound. It is not the case that a higher severity of injury or wound needs to be proved. The actus reus is identical, the same examples and case authorities included above for S.20 GBH can therefore be used as common across both offences.

Examples of GBH

There are many actions that could satisfy the actus reus of GBH. Some examples include:
- **Broken bones**
- **Stab wounds**
- **Bullet wounds**
- **Permanent injuries such as brain damage or disability**
- **Internal bleeding**
- **Loss of limb/s**
- **Psychiatric conditions**

It must still be established that the defendant factually and legally caused the injury to the defendant. You either need to establish that the defendant caused grievous bodily harm or a wound to the victim, applying exactly the same cases as considered for s.20.

Exam Gold In an application question if you have identified that the victim has suffered either GBH or a wound you know the offence you should be considering is either s20 or s18. When trying to establish which offence is the correct one for analysis you should focus ONLY on the mens rea of the defendant. The severity of the injury has no impact upon which is the correct offence for the defendant. It is not the case that serious injury is s20 and really serious injury is s18.

S.18 Mens rea

It is important to grasp the difference between the mens rea of s20 and s18 because this is the only factor that distinguishes the two offences when establishing liability.

The mens rea of a s18 offence can be satisfied in one of two ways:
1 **Intention to cause grievous bodily harm / to wound.**
2 **Intention to resist or prevent the lawful apprehension or detainment of any person.**

Either of these intentions will satisfy a s18 offence, it is not necessary to prove both. It is important to note that a s18 offence cannot be committed recklessly, therefore in order to establish liability it may be necessary to rely upon the principles of indirect intention developed in **R v Woollin (1998)** *(as discussed in chapter 2.)*

With regard the transmission of disease to another it is possible to be convicted of a s18 offence where the transmission to another is intentional.

Key Terms – Non-fatal Offences Against the Person

Assault	An act causing the victim to apprehend the infliction of immediate unlawful force on their person, committed with intention or recklessness as to causing such apprehension.
An act	The use of the phrase 'act' within the actus reus of assault indicates that the offence cannot be committed by omission.
Apprehension	As a result of the defendant's act the victim expects or anticipates that force is going to be used against the immediately.
Immediately	For the actus reus of assault it must be proved that the victim apprehend force in the immediate future or did not know what the defendant was going to do next but feared that it was of a violent nature.
Battery	The actual infliction of unlawful force against another with intention or recklessness as to the infliction of force.
Unlawful force	For the offence of battery, it must be proved that the defendant applied force, any slight amount will suffice, that they had no legal right to, either directly or indirectly.
Actual bodily harm	The phrase bodily harm is an ordinary phrase meaning, it 'includes any hurt or injury calculated to interfere with the health or comfort' of the victim. Further 'Such hurt or injury need not be permanent, but must, no doubt, be more than merely transient and trifling'.
Grievous bodily harm	Serious harm, this may be physical or psychiatric. It is not necessary for harm to be permanent or require treatment for this threshold of seriousness to be met.
Wound	A break in the continuity of the whole of the skin that cannot be proved by internal bleeding alone.

One Sentence Case Summary – Non-fatal Offences Against the Person

Name	Topic Link	Legal significance
Collins v Wilcock (1984)	Assault – actus reus	The actus reus of assault is '… an act which causes another person to apprehend the infliction of immediate, unlawful, force on his person'.
Tuberville v Savage (1669)	Assault – an act	There is no assault where the declares to the victim they are not going to carry out a threat against them. Words can negate an assault.
R v Ireland (1997)	assault – an act	Lord Steyn confirmed that silent phone calls can constitute an assault where it causes the victim to apprehend fear. Proximity of the defendant and victim is irrelevant, fear can be induced over the telephone.
R v Logdon (1976)	Actus reus – apprehension	A defendant may be guilty of assault despite the fact that the did not have the means nor intent of carrying out any threat.
Smith v Chief Constable of Woking Police Station (1983)	Actus reus - immediacy	Even where a threat cannot be carried out in that very moment, there may still be an assault if the victim does not know what the defendant is going to do next, but fears that it is of a violent nature and will be carried out in the very near future.
Collins v Wilcock (1984)	Battery – actus reus	The actus reus of battery is '…the actual infliction of unlawful force on another person'. Any touching of another can amount to a battery, however slight that touching is. There are many examples of touching in everyday life that are not a battery because they are lawful, for example by moving within society we impliedly consent to touching associated with that e.g., whilst in a busy supermarket or in a busy underground station.

One Sentence Case Summary – Non-fatal Offences Against the Person

Name	Topic Link	Legal significance
Haystead v Chief Constable of Derbyshire (2000)	Battery – application of force	The actus reus of battery does not require the direct application of force to the victim from the defendant to the victim, force that is caused to be applied indirectly e.g., via the medium of another person is sufficient to satisfy the actus reus.
Wilson v Pringle (1986)	Battery – application of force	The court confirmed that battery must be intentional and hostile touching. Also confirmed that acting in self-defence would amount to lawful touching.
Misalati (2017)	Battery – application of force	Spitting on another and make contact is sufficient to satisfy the actus reus of battery.
R v Donovan (1934)	Actual bodily harm – actus reus	The phrase bodily harm is a phrase that should take its ordinary meaning, it 'includes any hurt or injury calculated to interfere with the health or comfort' of the victim. Further 'Such hurt or injury need not be permanent, but must, no doubt, be more than merely transient and trifling'.
R v Chan Fook (1994)	Actual bodily harm – psychiatric harm	Actual bodily harm is not limited to physical conditions, it can also include psychiatric harm, however 'it does not include mere emotions such as fear or distress nor panic, as such, states of mind that are not themselves evidence of some identifiable clinical condition'.
R v Ireland (1997)	Actual bodily harm – psychiatric harm	The term 'bodily' in s47, s20 and s18 offences against the persons act 1861 is interpreted to include psychiatric injury.
R v D (2006)	Actual bodily harm – psychiatric harm	Psychiatric injury cannot amount to bodily harm for the purposes of non-fatal offences against the person, it must be proved that there is a recognisable psychiatric illness.
R v Abbas (2009)	Actual bodily harm – actus reus	Loss of consciousness is evidence of harm sufficient to amount to actual bodily harm.
DPP v Parmenter (1992)	Actual bodily harm – mens rea	The mens rea of a s47 offence is the mens rea of the initial assault or battery, for conviction it does not need to be proved that the defendant intended or was reckless as to any actual bodily harm occurring.
R v Saunders (1985)	Grievous bodily harm- actus reus	Grievous bodily harm requires proof of 'serious harm.
R v Dica (2004	Grievous bodily harm – actus reus	Knowingly or recklessly transmitting a serious sexual disease to a person who the risk is concealed is equal to s20 grievous bodily harm.
R v Golding (2014)	Grievous bodily harm- actus reus	Recklessly infecting another with a sexual disease may be guilty of a s20 offence, it is not necessary that the harm to be permanent, dangerous or even require treatment for this offence to be proved, further whether injury is sufficient to amount to grievous bodily harm is a matter for the jury to decide.

One Sentence Case Summary – Non-fatal Offences Against the Person

Name	Topic Link	Legal significance
R v Bollom (2004)	Grievous bodily harm- actus reus	When determining if injuries amount to serious harm, the particulars of the victim should be considered, this may involve reference to their age, health and effect of the harm upon the individual victim.
JJC v Eisenhower (1983)	Wounding – actus reus	For a wound to be proved there must be a 'break in the continuity of the whole of the skin', this means both the outer and under layers of the skin.
DPP v Parmenter (1992)	S20 mens rea	The mens rea of a s20 offence can be satisfied by proof of intention or recklessness as to some harm.

NOTES

For more help and support in OCR A-Level Law, scan the QR Code above.

www.tutor2u.net/law

OCR | A-Level | Law
SKU: 07-4130-30424-03 | ISBN: 978-1915610126

X001MFBFSV
OCR A Level Law Criminal Law Study Books
New